How to Leave Your Parents' Home and Live on Your Own:

A Guide for Teenagers and Young Adults

Montgomery Stewart

Stewart Consulting & Publishing, Inc.

Other books by the author:

The Nature of Power Struggles

Available from Amazon.com, CreateSpace.com and other retail outlets.

How to Leave Your Parents' Home and Live on Your Own: A Guide for Teenagers and Young Adults

Book Cover designed by prodesignsx at Fiverr.com

Library of Congress Control Number: 2016908757
Stewart Publishing, Hazel Crest, IL

ISBN-13: 978-0692722411 (Stewart Publishing)

ISBN-10: 0692722416

Dedication

To all the teenagers and young adults who are excited about leaving home but somewhat overwhelmed and confused about how to make it happen.

Acknowledgments

I would like to thank Charlotte Keys for her editing and consulting services on this project.

Contents

Introduction

This is a guide for parents, teenagers, and young adults to discuss and plan the inevitable transition of a young person moving out of the house to live independently. If a teenager or young adult does not have parents or someone to discuss this transition with, then this book can serve as an independent study guide to help that person live on his or her own. Certainly, parents have a responsibility to assist their children in becoming self-sufficient adults. However, due to various circumstances, some parents are better prepared or willing to help their children than other parents. For some parents or for a single parent, just surviving is all they can do, and preparing their children is beyond their abilities and means. In the end, if you are the teenager or young adult in this situation, you are responsible for yourself, whether that is right or wrong. I have written this book to provide a framework to help you think about how to live on your own as you move out of childhood and into adulthood.

The transition is smoother if you have been prepared and trained for this major life change. High school and life experience do not necessarily prepare the young person for this transition. In general, the teenager knows he or she wants to get an apartment, buy a car, and do all the things an adult does; however, wanting something and knowing the best way to get it are not the same. Living on your own does not require an extraordinary degree of skill, but it does require diligence. In this area, as with most things in life, it is easy to learn and master something if you are properly informed and trained. Without being taught, many will go through needlessly painful and expensive trial and error. Some will not succeed because they did not get the training they needed.

The best situation is for the parent(s) to work with the teenager to discuss next steps after graduating from high school. In general, high school graduation is a turning point or milestone in the teenager's life. Before graduation, the teenager should have been thinking about his or her next steps. After graduation, the teenager must start moving in some direction. Some of you will go to college, and others will join the armed services. Some of you will work entry-level, and/or low-paying jobs just to get started. Others will have an idea of the career they want to pursue and will look to start a job in that field. Some will even start a business. Of course, you can both work and go to school. There are many paths you can take to get started on the journey to living on your own.

In this book, the phrase "young adults" is used to include the group of individuals still living with their parents and trying to determine how to move out on their own. This will include teenagers in high school, high school graduates, and dropouts thinking about their next moves. This also includes adults living at home who, for various reasons, have not taken the steps to live on their own.

The Use of Internet Searches in This Book

The Internet is a powerful research tool. Everything that I discuss in this book you can research further by using the Internet. You can now access the Internet by mobile devices, including your smartphone. According to comScore.com and various other sources, as of 2014, more people access the Internet by mobile devices than by desktop computer. This means that accessing the Internet for your research purposes is a low hurdle to overcome. With more businesses, government institutions, restaurants, schools, and hotels offering free Wi-Fi (wireless Internet access), you can access the Internet for no cost.

Google is the dominant and most successful Internet search engine. All of the search examples provided in this book comes from Google. However, if you have problems locating the information you need, you should also use bing.com or other search engines. This method can only widen your search and help you gather more information. The challenge of finding information to assist young adults in moving out on their own is not a lack of information—there is more information than you can digest—but preventing yourself from becoming overwhelmed by all the information you discover.

One thing I want the young adult to get out of this book is that you can research on the Internet most questions you have about moving out on your own. You can find an apartment or a job and research colleges and employers, as well as educational requirements for various professions and vocations, the armed forces, and how to start a business. You can take classes through online colleges.

There is an abundance of information for self-study on numerous topics. There are also a variety of associations, study groups, and professional networks that you can join on a multitude of subjects. You can also find and share information with people who have similar interests. You should use this tool and information to your advantage.

For most of the issues I address related to moving out on your own, I have provided sample searches and results. These are just examples, but they are practical and useful. However, you can tailor your searches to meet your specific needs. It is helpful to bookmark useful websites in your browser for later use and referral. To keep yourself organized, create bookmark folders by subject matter, such as personal finance, schools, apartments, and cars, or use whatever names make sense to you.

When you find reports you'd like to download, save them to your hard drive or use a free document storage website, such as Google Drive or Dropbox. Google Drive currently provides fifteen gigabits of free storage, and it can be easily accessed from Google's Chrome browser.

Free Software

There is an abundance of free software on the Internet. Most young adults just starting out are short on cash. Free software will not have all the functionality of paid software, but it will adequately assist you in managing this project of moving out on your own and staying self-sufficient. If you use the Google Chrome browser, it will provide you with a tab underneath the search bar that has many of Google's free software applications (apps) and services. I used Google Sheets, a free Google Chrome app, for the spreadsheets contained in this book as a way of demonstrating the use of free software to help you stay organized. Google also has a web store with an abundance of free software, including finance and budgeting software. Although this book does not contain any budgeting software reviews, you can evaluate the free software available for yourself to see which will be most useful for managing your finances.

Mind-Set and Attitude

Your ability to succeed at the things you do and that you want to accomplish is in large part determined by your mind-set and attitude. You have to believe you have the ability to accomplish what you want. If you don't currently have that belief, then you must develop it along with the determination and persistence required to make things happen for yourself. Everyone is lacking something. Every dream is made from a desire to have something you currently lack. Tony Robbins, a famous motivational coach, has said that "It's not the lack of resources; it is the lack of resourcefulness that stops you."

How do you get from nothing to something? Different people have different approaches to this question. But, for the purposes of this book, I advise that you take a vague idea and make it clear and definite. For example, a vague idea is "I want my own apartment." You make it clear by determining whether you want a studio, one-bedroom, or two-bedroom apartment. In which community do you want that apartment? How much does that apartment cost? How much do you have to earn to afford that apartment? If you are new to the job market, you must ask yourself, "What kind of job will pay me what I need to afford that apartment and that car?" If you have a clear idea of your career path, then you must ask, "How can I earn the money I need from the living I have chosen to make?"

Let me give you an example of two people, David and Tony, one whose lack of resources will stop his efforts, and one who successfully uses the resources available to him. These two individuals think they want to become graphic artists. Neither has any experience, equipment, or software. This is just a vague idea that seems interesting. Both of these individuals became interested in this area from reading magazines (in print or online) and from seeing advertising with exciting graphics, bold fonts, and innovative artwork. They asked the questions, "How do you create something like that, and can I do that for a living?"

After some investigation, they discover that there are several paths in which to enter this field: a college degree, certifications, or learning on the job as an apprentice. Also available is self-study through which an artwork portfolio is created. There are successful graphic artists who have taken each path, and some of these paths can be taken in combination.

All of this is very exciting, but it also seems very overwhelming. You may need a college degree, or a high-end computer with costly specialized software, or a digital camera. Apprentice jobs at an advertising agency or graphic shop are not easy to come by. Let's say that David has only a smartphone and concludes that he needs an expensive new computer with expensive software. He hasn't quite given up, but he is not sure how to make this happen.

Tony has done some similar research, but he has decided to take small steps to move forward. He buys a used computer and installs a more powerful graphics card. His research has told him that the most common software in the industry is Adobe Creative Suite, but there is a graphic suite by CorelDRAW that is less expensive. In addition, there is Microsoft Publisher, which is inexpensive and will allow him to learn about layout and design. He is not a high-end professional yet, so he will take what he can get to start creating something for his portfolio. He decides he cannot afford new software, but there is plenty of less expensive used software. In fact, the Adobe website offers some low-end consumer software for free, which he can use to get started. He finds several shareware and freeware websites with a variety of graphic programs and tools that he can access for free in order to study his craft. He downloads these programs and begins learning how to use them.

I can take this example further by explaining how Tony begins to offer free business flyers and other graphic work to gain experience. But hopefully you can see where this is going. This is a simple example, but it illustrates a difference in mind-set and attitude. Tony did not have any more money or resources than David. But Tony was a lot more resourceful in getting the things he needed to move toward his dream.

One benefit of the Internet is that you can learn about the career you are interested in pursuing. You can find articles on successful people in that industry that describe how they became successful. You can find inspiration. You can use all of this to add clarity and definition to your vague idea. As your dream becomes clear, you will determine the appropriate next steps to take.

All of this may or may not happen within your specified time frame. But if you are determined and persistent, more positive things will happen. Tony had a more resourceful approach than David, who waited for the best circumstances, such as a new computer with the latest version of the best-known software. Please note that I am not saying that it's never appropriate to wait for the best circumstances. The point here is that you must ask yourself frequently whether you are being resourceful or whether you are stalled because you're focused on the obstacles and not the goal. Focus on your goals and how to move forward.

Let's get started on how to think about moving out on your own.

Chapter 1: What Are Your Options for Moving Out on Your Own?

There are certain things you need to know, regardless of the path you take, because you will have bills to pay. However, the path you take when leaving home will direct your efforts.

In this chapter, we will look at the standard paths available to young adults when leaving home, excluding getting kicked out of the house. If you find yourself in the situation where being told to leave the house is just around the corner, considering these options is still valid; you just won't have a lot of preparation time. For young adults, the standard options after high school are:

- Going to college
- Joining the armed services
- Getting a job
- Starting a business

Going to College

College is one path you can take as a means of moving out of your parents' home while getting an education. You can consider it an interim step between moving out on your own and living on your own. There are several different situations involved. Many parents will pay for their children's college education, so this step is not quite the same as the young adult moving out on his or her own and becoming independent. However, the move to college is one step toward independence.

If you are going away to college and paying your own way, then it is similar to moving out on your own. The only difference is that you are attending school full time and potentially working part time. Some young adults will attend school full time but live at home because the college is close to their parents' home, and living at home is more affordable and convenient. No matter the path, the following discussion will apply to all of these situations.

There are many types of colleges and universities. For example, I live in the Chicagoland area, which has more than twenty-five universities and fifteen colleges granting bachelor and graduate degrees. There are also more than twenty community and junior colleges. I found this information using Wikipedia (see https://en.wikipedia.org/wiki/List_of_colleges_and_universities_in_Chicago); you can conduct similar searches of your own hometown. The good news is that there are plenty of opportunities and choices in terms of getting a college degree as well as in terms of costs and areas of study.

When people complain about the high cost of a college education, they are usually focused on the top prestigious schools. Two examples in Chicago of expensive and competitively academic schools include Northwestern University and the University of Chicago. There is nothing wrong with aspiring to obtain a degree from such an institution. However, if you want to attend college and are concerned about the costs and the academics, you must find a college that fits your needs. Your job is to get clear about what you want to study and then find a college that has a program that meets your needs. This is not directed at only those who live in Chicago. Anyone in the United States can attend a college in another state. That effort may take longer to research, plan, and execute, but you can make it happen if you are committed to that course of action. Let us put aside location for a moment, which is a serious consideration, especially if you live in a rural area with limited options, and focus on more general needs.

The main thing about going to college is having an idea of what you want to study. You want to attend a school with a major that you are interested in pursuing. There are many college students who don't know what they want to study, and they use college to sort out what they are interested in pursuing. That approach is fine if you want to have a broad college experience. Moreover, if your only option is working in a burger joint managing the fry machine, then sowing your wild oats in college may not be a bad alternative. However, if that guy on the fry machine is learning the burger business with a plan to purchase several McDonald's franchises, then that is a man working on his career plan. The point is that it is acceptable to go to college for the experience, but there are other valid alternatives, especially when you are not sure what you want to study. However, let's focus our discussion on finding a college that has what interests you.

Visit College Websites

To help you realize what you might want to study in college, visit the websites of schools you think you want to attend. Study their information, as well as the majors they offer. I attended DePaul University (www.depaul.edu) in the 1970s (websites weren't available in those days), so I will use that as an example. DePaul's current website provides a list of majors and their concentration areas, along with a list of requirements and a schedule of classes. You can download these class schedules if that makes sense for you. Contact information is provided for program inquiries, and you can also apply online.

Many schools allow you to take classes as a non-degree-seeking student. This allows you to take a class to see how you like the school environment and potential major without worrying about committing to either. "Auditing" a class means you will not receive a grade and may or may not have to complete all of the work assignments to remain in class; it also means that you can test out the experience without worrying about a grade. In addition to information about the school's majors, there is information regarding:

- Admission requirements
- Financial aid
- Job opportunities, including internships

You also can apply for financial aid online or schedule a visit so that a staff member or volunteer can show you the campus and answer your questions. The contents of college websites will vary, but most will include similar information. Given that you can research college websites from your home or a library, there is every reason to take advantage of this information. From there, you can compare each school's online information. Note that DePaul University's website also provides online classes. This is not unique to DePaul, so check out this aspect of school life as well, as it may save you travel time and money.

If you know your career path already, find a school that offers that major and examine the environment to see whether it fits your personality. While you research, also investigate the financial aid available to you. This is still possible even if you don't know your career path. You can take a couple of courses to see whether the potential major is as interesting as you thought; if it's not, you can change direction before spending time and money studying that subject. This is one method you can use to gain clarity about attending a college that fits your needs while also finding a major to study.

To put this in a broader context, let me go back to the example of Tony and David, who were thinking about becoming graphic artists. In the example, they already have an idea of a major to study. Thus, Tony and David can research schools offering that degree. As part of that research, they can look at the available courses for various types of careers within the field. They can even attend classes to see whether this is the route they want to take in pursuing their careers. If they like the courses, they can pursue a degree in graphic arts design as part of their career paths.

If for some reason college does not work out, they can assess whether they still want to pursue a career as graphic artists, and if not, look at some other endeavor. Or maybe they still want to become graphic artists, but college was not the right path for them in pursuing that career. Perhaps some other training, such as a special art or computer school, for example, would be a better choice. Or maybe they skip a formal education for now and pursue an on-the-job apprenticeship or continue self-study and start freelancing. You are not going to finish everything you start, and not because you are a quitter. Persistence is important. However, your research will sometimes lead you to the conclusion that something you thought was interesting is, upon review, not worth pursuing. You live in a time where new industries are being created that did not exist ten years ago. For example, social media websites are now major job creators. Online commerce (shopping from a website) has reached critical mass, and many people are becoming self-employed by selling goods and services online. Aerial drone use for commercial purposes is a growing industry. Artificial intelligence applications are now being used in many industries. These rapid changes mean that, as old industries and career paths are fading out, new industries and careers are being created. There are a lot of opportunities today for someone who is staying abreast of current events, technologies, and social changes and looking to participate in these changes. It is your job to find out where you fit in all of these changes.

Joining the Armed Services

Joining the armed services is a path to leaving your parents' house if you are not college bound or do not have immediate job prospects. When I speak of the armed services (within the United States), I am referring to:

- US Army: www.army.mil and www.goarmy.com
- US Navy: www.navy.mil and www.navy.com
- US Air Force: www.af.mil and www.airforce.com
- US Marine Corps: www.marines.mil and www.marines.com
- US Coast Guard: www.uscg.mil and www.gocoastguard.com

The armed services can serve as both a goal and a means to an end. What do I mean? There are immediate benefits to serving these institutions, and there are benefits to you after you leave the service. For example, if you want to go to college but don't have the money or other resources now, you can obtain financial aid for college as a benefit of having served in the military.

The Immediate Benefits

- You have a job for which you are paid a salary with benefits, such as medical insurance.
- You have housing and meals.
- You can get an education and technical training.
- You can get job-related experience useful in your later job search.
- You can travel.

After You Leave the Service

- College education funds will pay for college and job training.
- You can get a mortgage for a house with your veteran's benefits.

A great source of information regarding the armed forces is the website military.com. The armed services are not for everyone. These are highly regimented institutions. There is a command structure based on rank, and you must take orders. There is also the downside of finding yourself in a war zone and becoming seriously and permanently injured. Some branches of the armed services are more dangerous than others.

However, between the online information available today and talking with current military personnel or veterans, you have the ability to learn whether this is an option for you to consider. If you are not sure about your next steps in moving out of your parents' home, you should investigate joining the armed services as a means to starting your life as an adult. Ask your sources for the real story, not the public relations version, and listen to your gut. Everything is not for everyone. Remember, too, that you must meet various requirements to join the armed services, so be sure to examine these as part of your research. The armed services can be a great and honorable career; just be sure it's the right one for you.

Getting a Job

In today's job market, most people will work many jobs over their lifetimes. It is possible to get a job paying an income that can meet your needs without a college degree. However, if you must consider a low-paying, entry-level job in order to move out of the house, do not despair. This is just a job to get you started; it is not a career. Many of you will have to take a low-paying, and/or entry-level job to make this transition and to learn how to live independently. That is why people go to college or get some other type of training—so that they can earn more income. Getting the training that makes sense to you will help you find a job or career that provides a sense of fulfillment beyond earning a paycheck. However, there is nothing wrong with just earning a paycheck. In fact, it is necessary in order to leave your parents' house and live on your own, unless that job cannot pay your expenses. However, most jobs will also help you get work experience in terms of:

- Dealing with people: managers, coworkers, and customers
- Learning skills that have value in the job market
- Helping you see and experience the types of jobs that may interest you

Jobs fall into several categories, see the list below. Starting with these categories will focus your search:

- Full-time salaried employment
- Full-time hourly worker
- Temporary worker employed through an employment agency
- Employee working on commission

Full-Time Salaried Job

With this type of job, you earn a yearly salary. For example, let's say for someone starting out of high school with limited skills, you are making $20,000 a year, which is effectively $10 an hour for a forty-hour workweek. As a full-time salaried employee, most companies will provide you with some level of benefits, but you must confirm what those are. Benefits can include:

- Medical, dental, and vision insurance
- Life insurance
- Paid vacation time
- Retirement plans, such as a 401(k)
- School tuition reimbursement
- Pension plan (becoming very rare these days)
- Discounts for specific goods and services

These are just some examples of the types of benefits associated with being a salaried employee. The type and quality of the benefits vary with each company, so do your research. Many larger companies will provide some information on employee benefits on the corporate website. Typically, if you are required to work more than forty hours a week as a salaried employee, you do not get overtime, as an hourly employee would.

Full-Time Hourly Employee

As an hourly employee, your income is determined by your hourly pay rate. For example, you could make ten dollars an hour, eight dollars an hour, or twenty-five dollars an hour. In this example, we are talking about being a full-time employee, which means working a forty-hour week. If you work more than forty hours a week, you are entitled to overtime, which is typically at a higher hourly rate, such as time and a half, which is fifteen dollars an hour if you make ten dollars an hour. A full-time hourly employee can have some of the same benefits previously discussed for salaried employees.

Temporary Worker (Also Known as a Contingent Worker)

An employer can hire a temporary worker directly or use an employment agency. If you work for a company through an employment agency, you are an employee of that agency and not the company for which you are performing services.

Many employment agencies have both a permanent placement department and a temporary placement department. The permanent placement department finds a worker a job and normally charges the company a fee. The temporary department finds jobs for temporary workers for many of the same companies.

Temporary work is associated with special projects, and once the project is completed, your job as a temporary worker has ended. That temporary job can last two days, two weeks, two months, or two years. It is possible to join a company as a temporary worker, make a good impression on the employer, and then have the employer offer you a permanent full-time position. Getting a job through an employment agency offers a way to work for a company without being hired, see if you like the company, and potentially obtain a full-time permanent position.

Some companies will hire a potential permanent full-time employee through an employment agency on a trial basis to see if things work out. If they do, the employer will make an offer of employment to the worker and pay the agency a fee. If things do not work out, the employer will end the assignment and look for another candidate. Temporary work has generally been associated with office work, but there are temporaries that support companies and industries for non-office work. If you are looking for work to move out your parents' house or to save the money to make such a move, then you should also investigate working for an employment agency.

You can use the Internet to search for employment agencies in your area. You can search by area code, but I am going to give you an example by using a city, Chicago, as the search area. I used the search phrase "temporary employment agencies in Chicago." Remember, you can make your search very broad or very specific. Here are the first five results:

City Staffing: Staffing Agency | Chicago Employment
citystaffing.com/ ▾
City Staffing is an award winning, staffing agency in Chicago specializing in temp, temp to permanent, and direct hire job placement services to a number of ...
View Available Positions - Apply Now - eConnect Portal Applications - Associates

Best Temp agency in Chicago, IL - Yelp
www.yelp.com/search?find_desc=**Temp+Agency**...**Chicago**%2C ... ▾ Yelp ▾
Reviews on Temp agency in Chicago, IL - City Staffing, The Chicago Hire Company, The Larko Group, Smart Resources, 24 Seven, Advanced Resources, The ...

Best Temporary employment agencies in Chicago, IL - Yelp
www.yelp.com/search?...**Temporary+Employment+Agencies**...**Chica** ... ▾ Yelp ▾
Reviews on Temporary employment agencies in Chicago, IL - City Staffing, The Chicago Hire Company, 24 Seven, Temp Time, The Larko Group, Advanced ...

Temporary Employment Agencies in Chicago, Illinois with ...
www.yellowpages.com › Chicago, IL ▾ Yellowpages.com ▾
Results 1 - 30 of 213 - Find 213 listings related to Temporary Employment Agencies in Chicago on YP.com. See reviews, photos, directions, phone numbers and ...

Temporary Employment Services & Staffing Agency | Elite ...
www.elitestaffinginc.com/ ▾
Elite Staffing provides temporary staffing and employment services to workers across a wide variety of industries. Find workers or look for a job today.

I also did a search using the phrase "temporary employment agencies in Chicago for high school graduates," which returned 4.4 million results on Google. Here are the first five results:

Graduate Jobs, Employment in Chicago, IL | Indeed.com
www.indeed.com/q-**Graduate**-I-**Chicago**.-IL-**jobs**.html ▼ Indeed.com ▼
Jobs 1 - 10 of 7169 - 7169 Graduate Jobs available in Chicago, IL on Indeed.com. one
search. all jobs. ... Craftsman Exhibits - Carpentry, Painting, Welding (Temporary. ...
and be a High School graduate or equivalent with participation in a relevant 50,000
employees located in more than 900 offices throughout the world.

For Student Jobs, Employment in Chicago, IL | Indeed.com
www.indeed.com/q-For-Student-I-**Chicago**,-IL-**jobs**.html ▼ Indeed.com ▼
Jobs 1 - 10 of 11683 - 11683 For Student Jobs available in Chicago, IL on Indeed.com.
one search. all ... Great for students, recent grads and others! .... Being a valet for us
is perfect for those looking for seasonal work, temporary work or for those looking for a
... Companies Currently Hiring: Moraine Valley Community College ...

No Experience Necessary Jobs, Employment in Chicago, IL ...
www.indeed.com/q-No-Experience-Necessary-I-**Chicago**.-IL... ▼ Indeed.com ▼
Jobs 1 - 10 of 2969 - 2969 No Experience Necessary Jobs available in Chicago, IL on
Indeed.com. one ... Ramp Service Employee - Temporary - Part-Time - United Airlines
- 835 reviews - Chicago, IL $11.48 an hour. NO AGENCIES PLEASE.

Temp Agency and Employment Service Jobs - Search and ...
www.**employment**guide.com/**Temp**%20**Agency**_... ▼ EmploymentGuide.com ▼
Create an online application to apply to Temp Agency and Employment Service ...
Most temporary jobs in this industry require only graduation from high school, ...

Jobs for High School Students - Employment Spot
www.**employment**spot.com/**employment**.../**jobs**-for-**high**-**school**-**students**... ▼
Temp Work may be a good summer job for high school students who are interested
... OfficeTeam and Manpower are two temporary agencies which offer some ...

At this point, you will need to make some phone calls and determine if it makes sense to set up an interview to discuss whether any of these employment agencies can help you find work. You may have to register with several companies as part of this process. Remember to look at temporary agencies as part of your search for a permanent full-time job.

Employees Working on Commission
Working on commission means you must sell something in order to get paid. Your commission (or income) is a percentage of the sales price. This is a customer-facing, customer service-type business where you sell a product or a service. You could have a job at the cosmetic counter at a retail store where you have to sell

makeup, perfume, and other products in order to earn a paycheck. You could work as a loan officer for a mortgage company selling mortgage loans to individuals who are buying or refinancing a house. You are paid when the loan is funded.

Some companies offer training programs and support while others don't. With this type of work, the higher the price of your product or service, the more your earning potential. This type of employment is another option to consider as you think about income potential to get the money you need.

Starting Your Own Business

Due to current technological advances, it is easier to start a business today than it was in the past, especially if you are entrepreneurially minded. However, trying to run a business is a full-time effort for most people—and often an expensive one. Right now, trying to move out of your parents' house in addition to living your current life requires all of your attention. Adding a business to this mix is not going to work out for the average person in your circumstances. I would advise that you consider running a business only after you are out on your own and settled. However, there are some individuals who may be able to juggle both efforts.

Organizing and Managing Your Job Search

Most likely, if you are looking for income, you are involved in a job search. Here are some things to consider when organizing and managing your job search:

- Perform research on the Internet.
- Develop your Resume and Cover Letters
- Use Self-Assessment Tests.

Internet Job Search

We have already talked about types of employment, so now let's discuss the actual job search. You can search for jobs by looking on the Internet:

- General job websites such as indeed.com
- Company websites such as homedepot.com
- Newspaper websites such as chicagotribune.com

- Municipal websites such as cityofchicago.org/jobs

By using these types of sites, you can sort job postings by industry, location, and salary, for example. You will find articles on how to write a resume and interview for a job, information on specific industries, degree and certification programs, and company information. These sites are a resource to educate you on the job market in general. Most major and midsize companies have their own websites. These are just examples. You can use Google, Bing, or your favorite search engine and type "job websites" to obtain more sites than you can effectively search.

What You Need: Resume and Cover Letter
In some cases, you may need a resume; in other cases, you may only need to complete an application, whether online or in person. If you are unsure of what is a resume, here is a definition I obtained from investopedia.com:

> A resume is a one to two page formal document that lists a job applicant's work experience, education and skills. A resume is designed to provide a detailed summary of an applicant's qualifications for a particular job—it is not usually meant to provide a complete picture. A good resume gives the potential employer enough information to believe the applicant is worth interviewing.

If you find a situation where you need a resume and a cover letter, once again there are samples on the Internet. Searching for "sample resume and cover letter for high school students" provided the following samples:

[PDF] Sample High School Resumes and Cover Letters
www.readwritethink.org/files/resources/30847_**sample**.pdf ▾
Page 1. Sample High School Resumes and Cover Letters. Page 2. Page 3. Page 4.

High school student sample cover letter | Career FAQs
www.careerfaqs.com.au › Careers › Sample Resumes & Cover Letters ▾
This free sample cover letter for a high school student has an accompanying high
school student sample resume to help you put together a winning job ...

Student Cover Letter Samples - Job Searching - About.com
jobsearch.about.com › ... › Sample Student Cover Letters ▾
Sample cover letters and cover letter templates especially for high school ... Cover
Letter Examples for High School and College Students and Graduates ... Writing
cover letters for resumes. including what to include in your cover letter, how to ...

[PDF] Student Cover Letters - A Way to Introduce Candidature
www.bths.edu/.../Preparing_a_**Student**_... ▾ Brooklyn Technical High School ▾
Most of us confuse between the resumes and these letters but the cover letters are
quite different from the ... 2. Sample Cover Letter For High School Students.

You can also take advantage of "self-assessment" tests that are designed to
determine your career interests and the current skills you have acquired to date.
The following is a list of free self-assessment websites I found using the search
phrase "job seeker self-assessment."

The Serious Job Seeker: 5.0 Self-Assessment: Don't leave ...
www.serious**jobseeker**.com/.../50-**self-assessment**-dont-leave-home.html ▾
Self-assessment is a big topic. And it's the one that you probably think you can skip.
But this is the heart and soul of the job search process for serious job ...

CareerSource: The CareerSource Process – Self-Assessment
www.careersourcenortheastflorida.com/**jobseekers**/.../**self_assessment**.asp... ▾
Job seekers can take a self-assessment to determine their strengths before beginning
your job search.

Self-Assessment for Job-Seekers Is First Step to Career Plan
www.quintcareers.com/career-direction/ ▾
Home » Self-Assessment for New Grads and Entry-level Job-Seekers Is First Step to
Career Plan. ... Each small step (short-term goal) will take you closer to satisfying the
big steps, known as long-term career goals. ... Navigate your future by performing a
self-assessment that will get ...

The Role of Self-Assessment | Monster.com
career-advice.monster.com › ... › Career Assessment ▾ Monster.com ▾
Self-assessment provides information about three important areas for career ... Values
are those key triggers you look for when searching for your dream job, ...

Self Assessments | CareerOnestop
www.careeronestop.org/.../**assessments**/**self**-**assessments**.a... ▾ Career One Stop ▾
Self-assessments can help you see what types of careers are likely to fit you. ... your
source for career exploration, training & jobs .... What is an assessment?

[PDF] Job seeker's guide - Groom & Associates
https://www.groomassocies.com/pdf/**jobseeker**_guide.pdf ▾
2. Part 1 – SELF ASSESSMENT EXERCISES. 1. Work values. 2. Interests. 3. Career
fields. 4. Skills inventory. 5. Occupational daydreams. Part 2 - JOB SEARCH ...

Self-Assessment | CareerFolk
www.careerfolk.com/tag/**self-assessment**/ ▾
My hunch is that a good number of job seekers give up in frustration. ... Finding a job is
about assessment and a level of self-exploration that you may not be ...

These self-assessment tests allow you to gain a better understanding of
your skills and goals. Many of us have an idea of what we want on a vague level,
but it helps to write down your thoughts and organize that information so that
you can get a clear picture of your skills and goals today.

Chapter 2: How to Plan for the Move Out of the House

In the last chapter, we talked about the common paths young adults normally take to live on their own. As you look for income and begin to plan your finances, you need an idea of how much money is required to make your move. This process allows you to organize your finances to support your plan. Let's look at the tools and methods you can use to get a picture of what you need to make your plans happen.

Organizing Your Finances to Live on Your Own

How Much Do You Need to Save?

You are going to need some money to make the actual move. I will use an example here that you can change to meet your needs. Let's assume that you want to move into a one-bedroom apartment in your area. We will talk about how to look for and evaluate an apartment in a later chapter. Here, we want to focus on how much money you need to move into a new apartment on your own.

You can use a pencil, paper, and calculator to perform these calculations. However, if you have access to a computer or mobile device, then you can use what is called an "electronic spreadsheet" and/or a software app. However, if money is limited, Google Docs are offered as part of the Chrome browser. The electronic spreadsheet in Google Apps is called "Google Sheets." If you have a copy of Microsoft Office, then you can use Microsoft Excel. Because Google Sheets is free and available on Chrome, which is also free, let's use this spreadsheet in our example.

Google Apps appears in the upper left-hand corner of the Chrome web browser. When you click the button, a page will open and display several Google Apps icons, including the green icon labeled "Google Sheets." Clicking on this icon takes you to another page with sample spreadsheets, and there is a blank spreadsheet you can open to create the following examples. There are sample budget spreadsheets you can use. However, for our purposes, the following spreadsheet will explain:

- How to create your own spreadsheet
- How the spreadsheet works
- How to use certain function icons to automate the work

Here is a simple spreadsheet for moving costs that I created in Google Sheets:

	A	B	C	D	E
1	Expenses		Costs		Comments
2					
3	Downpayment on Apartment		$1,000.00		First month rent and security Deposit
4					
5	Moving Van		$300.00		assuming you rent a truck, pay for gas, truck insurance, milage, boxes, tape & miscellaneous
6					
7	Deposits for Utiities		$300.00		With some apartment the rent includes utilities
8	Electricity				
9	Gas				
10	Cable				
11	Telephone				
12					
13	New Furniture and/or appliances		$500.00		
14					
15	Miscellaneous		$250.00		Renter's Insurance, credit check
16					
17	Total Expense		$2,350.00		

All of these costs are examples; you must research and calculate the cost associated with your own move into a new apartment. This sheet includes three simple columns. The first column includes the anticipated expenses based on your research. The second column is the cost or money you need to spend or to pay for the expenses identified in the first column. The third column is your comments and notes area, which you use to describe those expenses. Your job is to find out the expense and cost involved so that you know how much money you need to save or finance in order to move into your new apartment.

Most landlords will require the first month's rent in addition to a security deposit, which may equal the first month's rent. Here, I am estimating the monthly rent as being $500; therefore, the $1,000 in that column is the first month's rent plus a security deposit of the same amount. You will need to ask how much is required to move in. The purpose of the security deposit is to cover any damages to the apartment the landlord discovers after you move out. (Tip: taking pictures of your apartment while it is empty provides you with proof of the damage that existed before you moved in. This can help you avoid being charged later for damage you didn't cause.)

The second expense in the cost estimate is moving expenses. Once again, you must determine this cost. Your parents may help you move. You may not have enough furniture and belongings to rent a truck and several car trips will do the job. A friend with a van or truck may help you. However, if you have to rent a truck from U-Haul, for instance, additional fees will be attached to the rental cost. For example, you have to pay for mileage. How far are you moving? You have to pay for insurance to cover possible damage to the truck. You can rent the truck without this insurance, but if the truck is damaged during your move, you now have an additional expense—and it could be the full price of the truck. You will need boxes and packing supplies to move your things. These expenses are not difficult to estimate, but you need to take the time to create an estimate, as your job is to determine how much money you need to move. I used $300 for illustration purposes.

The third expense is for utility deposits. Some service providers will require that you provide a deposit in order to begin receiving services from them. Standard utilities are gas and electric. Cable or satellite is being replaced with Internet services, such as Netflix or Hulu. These are additional expenses you must think about: Are you paying for Netflix at home or is your mother? You may have your own cell phone, but are you paying that bill or are your parents? If you now need phone service, then get the cost associated with that expense and add it to this spreadsheet. You will have to determine what, if any, deposits are required for the standard utilities provided in your area. The $300 used for illustration purposes includes all of your utilities.

The next expense is furniture and appliances. Your parents may let you take your bed or bedroom set. You may have a table on which to eat your meals, or you may need to purchase these items. You may want a coffee pot, a few plates, glasses, and silverware. You may be able to get some of these or other items for free from family or friends. But you may have to buy a few things, too. Some can wait for later, but some you may need immediately; that is for you to decide. Once you determine what, if anything, you need to buy in this area, add it to the spreadsheet. I used $500 for illustration purposes.

Finally, I have a catchall expense of miscellaneous. This can include renter's insurance and a credit check fee. Some landlords will require a credit check and some will not. You can decide whether you want to buy renter's insurance now, wait for later, or just skip this expense. Basically, renter's insurance protects your possessions in case of fire or theft. Examine the insurance policy carefully to see what is covered.

We now have estimated total expenses of $2,350. In this example, that is how much you need to save or finance in order to move into a new apartment to get started living on your own. This is just the cost to acquire an apartment; it is not the monthly cost to maintain an apartment. You must create a budget to do that, which we will discuss in the next section, but you need to have an idea of that number (an estimate) also.

There are many websites you can look at to research this issue, as well as apartment living in general. I performed a sample Internet search on the phrase "living in your first apartment." Other phrases that came up were "tips for living in your first apartment," "living alone in first apartment," "first apartment living room checklist," and "first apartment essentials." The following are the search results for "living in your first apartment":

Frugal Tips for Millennials Moving Into Their First Apartment ...
www.bankrate.com/.../**first-apartment**-tips-for-millennials-1.asp... ▾ Bankrate ▾
Living with your parents or sharing a space with roommates can get a little ... But
there's a lot that can come along with moving into your **first apartment**.

Do's and Don'ts for Moving into Your First Apartment - Rent ...
www.rent.com/blog/moving-into-**your-first-apartment**/ ▾
Are you getting ready to move into your first apartment? ... These items are all
important parts of living alone, so check out apartment checklists to make sure you ...

25 Things Nobody Tells You About Your First Apartment
www.buzzfeed.com/.../things-nobody-tells-you-about-**your-first-apartme**... ▾
25 Things Nobody Tells You About Your First Apartment .... Speaking of living with
other people: Once you've pooled your worldly possessions, chances are you ...

Seven Things I Wish I Knew Before Getting My First Apartment
lifehacker.com/seven-things-i-wish-i-knew-before-getting-my... ▾ Lifehacker ▾
Feb 24, 2014 - Every time you rent an apartment, you learn something new that you did
... The first time you go off and live on your own—or at least away from ...

25 tips for living in your first off-campus apartment | Campus ...
college.usatoday.com/.../25-tips-for-**living-in-your-first**-off-campus-apar... ▾
Sep 24, 2014 - Do your homework prior to apartment shopping and you should be on
the right path to finally finding your dream dwelling.

First Apartment Tips - Huffington Post
www.huffingtonpost.com/news/**first-apartment**-tips/ ▾ The Huffington Post ▾
Tips On Finding Your First Apartment ... every twentysomething goes so they can fill
their most precious living quarters with affordable furnishings... that all of the.

My First Apartment: Ready To Move Out On Your Own?
www.my**firstapartment**.com/ ▾
Moving to your first apartment? ... In order to help My First Apartment readers, we
have now surveyed actual costs ... Living With Your Introvert/Extrovert Roomie.

I recommend that you perform a search using any of these phrases, or use
your own, and research what is involved in living in your first apartment. Now, let
us look at creating an expense spreadsheet to estimate how much it will cost you
to maintain an apartment.

Creating a Budget Using Google Sheets

The advantage of using Google Sheets is that once the budget is created, the totals will update automatically as you adjust each cost. Once the budget is set up, it becomes a time-saving device. In order to do this, you must use the sigma icon Σ. This symbol and function is found on the right side of the app by clicking the button labeled "More." The sigma symbol is the last symbol on the right-hand side in a group of symbols, as shown in the following toolbar image:

Click the down arrow on this icon and select SUM. This means that the cell where you insert the symbol will add up all the cells (and costs) you indicate within the parentheses ( ). In our example spreadsheet, the $1,000 cost for the apartment down payment appears in cell C3, and the last miscellaneous cost of $250 is in cell C15. The app automatically adds these cells with their costs in the "Total expense" cell. The formula for this calculation within the parentheses is (C3:C15). If you change the moving van cost from $300 to $600, the app will automatically adjust the total. This is the benefit of using a spreadsheet. If you get confused, you can always click on the "Help" button.

You can also create several scenarios in different columns. For example, you can create estimated costs for moving into different living situations, such as a studio, one-bedroom, or two bedroom apartment, and see the difference in cost. A sample spreadsheet of this comparison is provided in chapter 5. Therefore, spreadsheets are good for asking what-if questions and then seeing how things compare.

How Much Do You Need Each Month to Keep Your Apartment?

Creating a budget

There are several ways to create and format a budget. What I am going to show you is just one method. If you are reading this book on a computer, whether the type of computer is a mobile device, tablet, laptop, or desktop, then there is no reason not to use either an electronic spreadsheet or an app specifically designed for managing your finances. However, if for some reason you are using a pencil, paper, and calculator, then you can still create this budget. The following budget is basically an income and expenses statement for one month. The two dates provided represent two pay periods in a month, which is how many people are paid.

Income	1/1/2016	1/15/2016	Total	Comments
Job	$560	$560	$1,120	You make $10 an hour; after taxes, you bring home 70 percent of your total earnings.
Other				
Other				
Total income	**$560**	**$560**	**$1,120**	
Expenses				
Rent	$500		$500	
Food	$50	$50	$100	To some degree, you control this expense. What is the minimum you need for a two-week period?
Gas	$30		$30	With some apartments, gas is included in the rent, but if not, this is an expense that increases in the winter, especially if you live in the north or on the east coast.
Electric		$30	$30	Same as previous comment.
Cell phone and Internet		$60	$60	
Transportation	$60		$60	This assumes you take public transportation and are using a monthly bus or train pass.
Credit card			$0	
Insurance (car or renter's)			$0	
Medical, dental, vision			$0	
School			$0	
Clothing	$25		$25	This is a minimum amount, even if you have an adequate wardrobe.
Entertainment			$0	

Savings	$100	$100	$200	
Total expenses	$765	$240	$1,005	
Excess or (shortage)	−$205	$320	$115	You have a small excess at the end of each month after paying your bills.

Let us look at the working assumptions built into this budget. First, this budget assumes that you are working a job making ten dollars an hour and that you are working forty hours a week. It also assumes that you are paid every two weeks and bring home 70 percent of your gross paycheck after taxes, unemployment, and social security deductions. This also assumes that your employer is taking out these deductions. If that is not the case, then you are bringing more cash home, but you will also need to make these tax payments to the government, which is another topic altogether. You see that I have three lines for income. Many people work more than one job or do some other things to supplement their income; the possibility for other income is built into this situation.

In terms of timing, you must know what day of the month your bills are due. You are paid twice a month, but if too many bills are due in one pay period, then you may constantly pay a bill late. Paying bills late is not good for the credit history you are building. Arrange your bills so that you can meet your obligations without being late. For example, you can call a utility company and ask if you can pay your bill in the third week of the month, because you have to make that $500 rent payment on the first of each month. You can negotiate with your creditors.

The bottom right-hand corner of this spreadsheet shows that you have an excess of $115 each month, or $57 a paycheck. Although you can pay your bills, things are tight, and you need some additional income, because there is no room for mistakes or an emergency expense here. Let's examine and discuss each expense.

Rent. The first and biggest expense is your rent of $500 a month. This expense is 45 percent ($500 divided by $1,120) of your total monthly income ($1,120). Plus, you still have apartment-related expenses to pay, such as utilities. As you plan your move, you must think about whether you can get a cheaper place or how you can get additional income. This may mean a roommate to help you cover expenses, assuming that is an option for you. Not everyone wants a roommate.

Depending on which part of the country you live, $500 a month may only get you a studio apartment. In this case, you don't want a roommate because there is not enough room for two people, unless your roommate is your significant other. However, in some parts of the country, $500 will get you a roomy two-bedroom apartment. You must research and learn the rental market where you live.

Food. Right now, you are spending $100 a month for food, which is $25 a week or $3.57 a day. It certainly means you are taking your lunch to work. This is a low number for most people, so adjust the number to represent your needs.

Gas. This thirty-dollar gas bill is the utility bill to heat your apartment. Some apartments will provide heat as part of the rent you pay. This number can vary greatly depending on what part of the country you live in and the season. If you live where there are harsh winters, then your gas bill could easily go over a hundred dollars. If you have to pay for heat, you can always call the gas company, tell them where the apartment is located, and ask for the average monthly gas bill that has been paid previously so that you can get an estimate.

Electricity. This thirty-dollar bill brings the same issues as with gas, and you can always call the electric company and see what was paid in the prior year. You can also ask the landlord for the average cost.

Cell phone and Internet. Landline telephones are disappearing, and most young adults use cell phones. Most cell phone plans include a data plan, which means Internet access, and your assumed cost is sixty dollars. These days, most cell phones can be used as mobile hot spots, so you can access the Internet on your other devices, such as a laptop or tablet, using your cell phone as an Internet connection. You can price cell phone plans. Most of you will have cell phones already; the question is whether you are paying for it or your parent(s) are. If your parents are paying, will they continue to do so?

Transportation. This number (sixty dollars) assumes you use public transportation with a monthly bus or train pass. So this is a bare minimum number, unless you live within walking distance to your job. Of course, you may have a car. You may own the car outright or have a car loan. A car is more convenient, but it is also more expensive to acquire and maintain. With a car you have the following potential expenses:

- Car loan
- Car registration and insurance
- Gas
- Maintenance
- Parking

If you have a car or plan to buy (whether new or used) or lease a car, you must determine these costs and insert them into your budget.

Credit card. You should have a credit card for emergencies. A zero balance is recorded on our sample budget. However, you may have a credit card already with a balance. In that case, put your monthly payment on this row. Remember that it is easy to have a credit card and start buying shiny items you don't need, only to max out (spend to your credit limit) your card and make minimum payments each month. This is an easy mistake most people have made or will make. The problem with this abuse is that you maintain a high balance and interest rate because the minimum payment will not pay off the credit card. But just as important in terms of you being able to live on your own is that you have access to credit in case of an emergency.

Insurance. A zero balance is recorded here. However, you may want to purchase renter's insurance to protect your personal belongings in case of fire or burglary. If you can't afford it now, you may want to consider how to increase your income so that you can afford it at a later date. If you have a car, then you are required by law in most states to at least have liability insurance to protect the other driver in case of an accident, so you may have an expense here.

Medical insurance (or expenses). This includes medical, dental, and vision. For this example we have zero as the expense. If your employer provides insurance, then this is taken out of your check. Your employer will pay part of your insurance, but you will also pay for part of the monthly insurance payment.

If it is taken out of your check, you do not need an expense line item. However, you may not have employer-paid insurance and you may need to buy your own policy. Under Obamacare, or the Patient Protection and Affordable Care Act, everyone is technically required to have insurance. Regardless of the requirements of Obamacare, you are either going to secure your own medical insurance or set aside money to see the doctor, dentist, and eye doctor. You should determine whether you can afford medical insurance, and one place to begin your search is www.healthcare.gov. You currently have an extra $115 a month, which may buy you a minimal policy.

Even if you cannot afford medical insurance, you will periodically need to see a doctor or dentist. Many doctors' offices will see you without insurance for an office visit. Be sure to ask the question, "How much does it cost for an office visit if I don't have insurance?" Many doctors and dentists will charge less than a hundred dollars to examine you, discuss your symptoms, give you a physical, and write you a prescription if you need it.

Maybe you wear eyeglasses and need a new prescription periodically. Or perhaps you have a toothache and need to see the dentist. There are free clinics in many areas if you can't afford care. However, you will have to pay for some medical care during the year, even if it is the bare minimum. You can put some minimal number in the spreadsheet or keep this thought in the back of your head. To tie this item to savings, I would say this is in part what your savings account is for if you don't have medical insurance.

School. A zero balance is recorded here. School does not have to include college, but it can include any courses or activities that will increase your skill set so that you can make more money in the job market. When I say job market here, I mean either working as an employee or a freelancer or having a small business. Working as a freelancer is a form of self-employment. You don't necessarily need a diploma, but you may need a certificate or skill set you can demonstrate. As a young adult moving out on your own and looking at entry-level positions, you have to think about how you are going to increase your earning potential.

Clothing. This item assumes a minimum of twenty-five dollars a month. You will not buy clothing every month, but within a year you will need some additional things, such as winter shoes, a fall jacket, or the like.

Entertainment. A zero balance is recorded here; however, let's be realistic: you will want to periodically go out with friends or just to treat yourself. You control the cost, but understand there is a cost here.

Savings. This assumes $200 savings, so you are putting some money away every month and still have $115 available. Creating a savings plan is important. Many financial advisors will say you must pay yourself first, and I agree. However, you can't save money if you can't pay your basic expenses.

The primary reason it is important to have savings when you live on your own is to pay for unexpected expenses. Let's say your car breaks down and you need to have it towed. Towing is an expense. Let's assume the mechanic says you need a new radiator hose and it will cost $250, and the tow was $200. Now, if you have a credit card, maybe you can use that. But if you don't have a savings account or a credit card, then you have to borrow the money or you can't get your car repaired. Maybe there is no one who can or will lend you money. You may not be able to get to work without a car, so that causes further problems. Unexpected things happen in life, and when you are on your own, you need a way to manage them. That is why you need a savings account. But you must be able to pay your basic bills first. Going back to our earlier example, you could get an annual American Automotive Association (AAA) membership to cover towing expenses, but that will not cover automobile repairs.

This exercise is a planning tool. If you go through this process while you are living with your parents, you can see what is ahead and determine a way to manage it. It is recommended that you complete this planning stage now, before you move out, rather than after. However, if you are living on your own now and struggling, then you must go through this exercise to determine your next steps, such as where to cut expenses or how to increase your income. That is why I say the spreadsheet is a great what-if tool: you can change the numbers to look at your financial situation under different circumstances. What if I could decrease my rent by $150 and reduce my insurance by $50? What if I can earn an additional $500 per month? You can get a realistic picture of what you need to do in order to move out on your own.

Based on the numbers presented in our sample budget, I would conclude that you can pay the bills associated with a $500 monthly rent only making $10 an hour. Although you are able to save $200 per month, this is a challenge, but it may be a challenge you are willing to take on to start living on your own. However, you should think about how you can make an upgrade to your income, because your expenses are minimal, and it will be difficult to cut them.

Because your rent ($500) is 45 percent of your take-home income, you have less money available for your other expenses. Can you find a less expensive apartment that meets your needs? In this situation, you can't afford a car; but if you don't need one, then it doesn't matter. If you do need a car, then you need more income.

Of course, many people are in this situation, and some are managing while others are struggling. However, this situation is a learning experience and stepping stone. Remember, many people are working at jobs where they make only seven or eight dollars an hour, which is around the hourly rate of working at Walmart. Now, there are also people making twenty-five, forty, and sixty dollars an hour and more. But the average young adult between the ages of seventeen and twenty-four is not going to make that kind of money. It is not impossible, and there are many examples of young people making significant salaries. But for the average young adult reading this book, your life will be one of incremental upgrades, and your first upgrade is to move out on your own.

Backing into a required income level to upgrade your life. The next step in using a spreadsheet as a what-if tool is to ask the question, "How much do I need to earn in order to live at a certain level?" In other words, how much money do you need to make for your next desired upgrade?

You start by creating a spreadsheet and including all the payments you need to make in order to have what you want. You are looking at this from a monthly payment perspective, and we will then convert those monthly payments to a yearly number and answer the question, "How much money do I need to earn to pay for these items?"

Let's say you want to upgrade from a one-bedroom apartment to a two-bedroom apartment with two bathrooms. You do not have a car, but you want to buy a new car. You want to have full medical, dental, and vision insurance and put $500 a month in a savings account. Let's examine the following spreadsheet:

Expenses	1/1/2016	1/15/2016	Total	Percentage of expenses
Rent	$1,200	$0	$1,200	36.09%
Food	$150	$150	$300	9.02%
Gas	$75	$0	$75	2.26%
Electric	$0	$50	$50	1.50%
Cell phone and Internet	$60	$0	$60	0.15%
Car payment	$0	$350	$350	10.53%
Car insurance	$100		$100	3.01%
Gas and tolls	$60	$60	$120	3.61%
Car maintenance	$20	$20	$40	1.20%
Credit card	$0	$0	$0	0.00%
Renter's insurance	$30	$0	$30	0.90%
Medical, dental, vision	$0	$300	$300	9.02%
School	$0	$0	$0	0.00%
Clothing	$50	$50	$100	3.01%
Entertainment	$50	$50	$100	3.01%

Savings	$250	$250	$500	15.04%
Total expenses	$2,045	$1,280	$3,325	
Take-home monthly income			$3,325	
Take-home yearly income			$39,900	
Yearly income before taxes			$57,000	

For consistency with the previous spreadsheet, this one also uses the pay period format. You don't need it here because this example is less about payment timing and more about projecting income to support your vision of an upgrade. However, I am trying to teach you how to build your own spreadsheet to fit your needs. That is why I talk about assumptions, because when you generate your numbers, you will know the assumptions you are using. I will focus on the total column in discussing costs for each item. I have also added a percentage column so that it is clear which expenses is the largest and how much of your income they take.

Rent. The first item is apartment rental at $1,200, which is 36.09 percent of your total expenses. This expense is a lesser percentage of the prior estimated $500, which was 45 percent of your income. But this higher rent is a lower percentage only because there are so many additional expenses to support a higher lifestyle.

Food. This cost is now $300 a month, or $150 a pay period, for an average of $10 a day. This is your fourth largest expense at 9.02 percent.

Utilities. Your gas, electric, and phone utilities are $185 a month, and I suspect gas is underestimated. But once again, you can research these expenses for a specific apartment.

Car. Your second largest estimated expense is car related. A $350 car loan is 10.53 percent of your expenses. However, total car-related expenses include gas, tolls, maintenance, and insurance for a total monthly expense, including the car payment, of $610 per month. The total of these expenses is 18.35 percent. Once again, these are costs you can research and estimate for yourself, but you can see that having a car is a major expense.

Credit card. This new budget includes a credit card, but I did not add in an expense.

Renter's insurance. I listed renter's insurance for an average monthly cost of thirty dollars per month.

Medical, dental, and vision insurance. This is noted as a $300 monthly expense. Once again, this is something you must research, as this is just a rough estimate. This cost is equal to your food cost of $300, or 9.02 percent of your income. Also, given the income that is calculated, there is a significant chance you have employer-provided insurance. However, this assumes you are an employee and not self-employed.

School. This row includes any type of continuing education either for self-improvement or to upgrade or maintain your current skill set. A number has not been entered here, but you may have continuing education in your budget.

Clothing. The item is listed at $100 per month. This will vary with each individual and will change month to month.

Entertainment. This is also $100 per month. Once again, this is a number you must determine for yourself.

Savings. The final entry is savings at $500 per month. Savings is your third largest expense at 15.04 percent of your budget.

These estimates are just one way of answering the question, "How much do I need to earn in order to live at a certain level?" Create your own spreadsheet based on what you want. The total for this example on a monthly basis is $3,325. That is cash after taxes you need to make these monthly payments. The yearly amount is $39,900 ($3,325 x 12). This example assumes that you are paid by an employer who is deducting taxes, unemployment insurance, and social security from your check. It also assumes that you bring home after these deductions approximately 70 percent of your check. Under these assumptions, you will make a yearly salary of $57,000 ($39,900/.70).

If you have additional deductions taken from your check, such as a portion of employee-provided medical insurance, 401(k) retirement plan deduction, or savings, the numbers will change accordingly. Therefore, your net check or take-home pay is less than 70 percent. Once again, you must know the assumptions behind the numbers you are creating. This is how you can determine why you need to earn $57,000 annually for a two-bedroom apartment and a new car, as well as to save $500 a month and meet the other expenses in this example.

Remember that this is just an example, so don't let the $57,000 required income overwhelm you. Adjust the numbers until you come up with something you believe you can achieve and work with under the present circumstances.

How Do You Link Your Income Projections to Your Job Search and Education Plans?
Now that you know how much income you need for a certain lifestyle, the question becomes, "What can I do to earn this level of income?"

If you have not identified a career you want to pursue, then you need to search for jobs that pay at this income level. As part of this search, you must learn what type of education and experience you need to qualify for these jobs. If you have identified a career, then you need the income levels available within this career choice. If you can earn your projected income level, you need to determine at what level you need to progress in order to earn that income. For example, maybe you need to become a master carpenter before you can earn $57,000 a year, and in general it takes three years to obtain that level of experience and income. You can apply this thought process to any job or career.

Some career choices require a formal education, such as a four-year college degree, and other careers do not. Some careers require a certificate or certification to get started. Certifications are very common in the information technology industry, as are two-year technical degrees from institutions such as DeVry University. These and other schools also offer online training, so you can take classes from your apartment. And in this and other fields, it is possible to earn $57,000 with a two-year technical degree. There are also areas, such as writing software code, where you don't need a formal degree, and certification programs that allow you to obtain a higher paying job making $25 an hour and better. These are examples of what is available once you do some research on how to move forward in making an upgrade. Also review the discussion in chapter 1 regarding job search methods.

It is important to understand that a timing element is involved. Depending on your circumstances, moving from a studio apartment to a two-bedroom apartment may require an interim step of living in a one-bedroom apartment as you increase your income level. A move to your desired goal may take two years or five years. The point here is to tie your projections back to your research to earn more income. However, let's not get ahead of ourselves; you still have to move out of your parents' house first.

Chapter 3: Documents Needed to Manage Your Personal Affairs

In this country, you need formal documentation to identify yourself in order to take care of your business. Employers, schools, lenders, business partners, government agencies, and various other institutions will ask for your identification to validate your identity. In addition, these same institutions will run credit and security background checks on you. In order to achieve your goals, you must gather the most common documents and have them ready to present to these various institutions.

The following is a list of the most common documents requested, along with a website where you can research and obtain these documents if you don't already have them.

Birth Certificate

When Do You Need This Document?
- Many states require it to obtain a driver's license or state ID.
- Some states require it to get married.
- You need it to obtain a Social Security card.
- Some branches of the armed services require it.
- Some employers require it.
- You need it for a passport to travel outside the United States.
- It is good to have one to prove your citizenship and identification.

Where Do You Get This Document?
- Your parents may have a certified copy.
- Contact the hospital where you were born.
- Some states require you go to a specific office. For example, in Illinois, you can get a copy from the Illinois Department of Public Health.
- You can also go to the United States Department of Vital Records: www.usa.gov/replace-vital-documents.

Social Security Card

When Do You Need This Document?
Not everyone will ask to see the card, but many institutions will ask for your social security number (SSN).

- Most employers will request your SSN.
- You need your SSN for federal and state tax returns.
- Most financial institutions will ask for your SSN.
- Most insurance providers will ask for your SSN.
- Most lenders will ask for your SSN.
- Most schools require your SSN.
- Many service providers, such as your doctor and dentist, will ask for your SSN.

Where Do You Get This Document?
- You apply for an SSN through the Social Security Administration: www.ssa.gov/ssnumber/. You can also apply for a replacement card at this website.

Driver's License or State-Issued Picture ID

When Do You Need This Document?
- In most states, you need a state-issued driver's license to operate a motor vehicle. Many people also use their driver's licenses as picture IDs.
- Most employers will ask for a driver's license as a form of picture ID.
- If you don't have a driver license, you can obtain a picture ID from the state.

Where Do You Get This Document?
- Each state has its own requirement, so visit the local state Department of Motor Vehicles (DMV) office or go to the website. For example, Illinois's DMV website is the following: www.cyberdriveillinois.com/departments/drivers/drivers_license/home.html. Also for Illinois, I found a privately operated website that was more user friendly: www.dmv.org/il-illinois/apply-license.php. Your state may also have something similar.

Voter's Registration Card

When Do You Need This Document?
- You need this to vote in local, state, and national elections.
- It is a form of identification but not a picture ID.

Where Do You Get This Document?
I will use the state of Illinois as an example here, but you can do a search in your location to determine where to register to vote. Normally, you can find a municipal organization in which to register at the city, county, or state level. There are several options for registering in Chicago:

- You can obtain a voter's registration form to mail in at the State Board of Elections: www.elections.il.gov/votinginformation/voterregforms.aspx.
- You can register with the Chicago Board of Elections Commissioners: www.chicagoelections.com/en/grace-period-registration-and-voting.html.
- If you live in Cook County, Illinois, you can register with the Cook County Clerk's office: www.cookcountyclerk.com/elections/registertovote/pages/whereandhowtoregister.aspx.

Passport

When Do You Need This Document?
You typically need a passport to travel outside the United States. This can apply to air travel and boat cruises. If you travel to Mexico and Canada by land, you can use a passport card that looks like a driver's license and is less expensive than a passport.

Under the Real ID Act of 2005, some state-issued driver's licenses may be deemed inadequate for air travel, and as a result, your driver's license or state-issued ID will not be acceptable when boarding an airplane. As a result, you will need a passport or a passport card for domestic air travel.

The Homeland Security website (www.dhs.gov/current-status-states-territories) indicates that the following states were not complaint in terms of their state-issued IDs being adequate for air travel:

- Illinois
- Minnesota
- Missouri
- Washington

If you plan to travel by plane and you are using a state-issued ID from these states, you should call the airline you are flying to validate whether your ID will be accepted to board your flight. However, the bottom line is that you may need a passport more often for future domestic travel then you do today for foreign travel. Thus, having a passport or passport card will help to alleviate any problems with state-issued IDs.

Where Do You Get This Document?
- You can obtain a passport or passport card by completing an application and other information regarding requirement from the following website: www.us-passport-service-guide.com/proof.html.

Chapter 4: Managing Your Money and Financial Tools—Part 1

Savings and Checking Accounts

We have discussed the need to create and increase the size of your savings account. Look at it as an emergency fund to access when unexpected expenses arise. Many financial planners suggest that you try to create an emergency fund that encompasses six months of expenses. This is a goal you can strive to obtain. The first goal is to save one month of expenses. Of course, there are other things you can save for, including school, vacations, and major purchases. If you cannot afford a savings account, then you need to focus on upgrading your financial situation so that you can afford to save money.

Your basic options are to open a savings account with a bank or credit union. The savings account is a place to keep your personal savings for emergencies. You can also place money in a mutual fund to obtain a greater return than the interest that is paid on a savings account. However, your money is not insured from loss as it is in a bank or credit union savings account. You can put your savings in a US savings bond or certificate of deposit to potentially get a better rate, but you have to cash in the bond or certificate if you need to access the money. Other savings alternatives are beyond the scope of this book, but you can easily research them yourself. However, the easiest and most straightforward method is to keep your emergency fund in a savings account. Once you open an account and begin saving money, you can do some financial research to see whether there is a better alternative.

Because the plan is to save the money you need before you move out, you should set up a savings account before leaving your parents' house, if you do not have one already. Opening a savings account is easier than a checking account because you are not writing checks against the account. Therefore, you don't run the risk of an overdraft—that is, writing a check for money you do not have in your account. You are merely depositing money and withdrawing money.

The next step is to open a checking account with a bank or credit union to pay your bills. The advantages of having a checking account include the following:

- You have a centralized place to manage your finances.
- You can see your checking history and current balance online twenty-four hours a day from your computer.
- You can electronically move money between a savings account and checking account.
- You can check your account online for fraud.
- You can pay your bills online.
- You can make online purchases using your checking account debit card or checking account information through such services as PayPal.
- You are establishing a relationship with the bank in order to obtain other financial services later.
- In many cases, you can have your paycheck directly deposited into your checking account.

Some banks charge more for a checking account than others. However, with some effort, you should be able to find a bank that charges a reasonable monthly fee under fifteen dollars.

The alternative to a checking account with a bank or credit union is to cash your checks at the following locations:

- Currency exchanges
- Large retailers providing check-cashing services
- Local grocery stores providing check-cashing services
- The bank where the check was issued but where you are not a customer
- Payday lenders offering cash-checking services

There are numerous places that serve those who don't have bank accounts. However, a common reason why people cannot open a checking account is that they had one previously and it was closed involuntarily. In other words, the bank closed the account because it was mismanaged. Most young adults reading this book should not have that issue. If you do, then you need to go to the bank where you had the problem and see what you can do, if anything, to resolve the issue so that the bank will stop reporting your account as being closed due to a problem.

In general, these alternatives to checking accounts are more expensive, not because the check-cashing fees are higher than bank fees, which is possible, but because once you have cashed your check, you now need to pay your bills. With some creditors, you may go to an office to pay your bills, as with a utility. The currency exchange will also let you pay utility bills for a fee. Paying your bills via a money order issued from the post office will also incur a fee. If you are paying a check-cashing fee and a fee to pay each bill, those fees, in my experience, exceed the cost of maintaining a bank checking account. You can compare the fees for both alternatives as they pertain to your situation and decide which makes the most sense to you.

Some local grocery stores will cash your check, but you have to find somewhere else to pay your bills. Some large retailers, such as Walmart, offer check-cashing and bill-paying services, but as with currency exchanges, there is a fee for each bill you pay. I am not endorsing Walmart, but I am using it as an example, so if you want to see the fees involved and compare those to a local currency exchange and bank, visit the following website: www.walmart.com/cp/Check-Cashing/632047.

You can always take your payroll check to the bank where your employer has its checking account on which the check was written. Some banks may refuse to cash your check if you are not a customer. Many banks may either offer to open a bank account for you as a new customer or advise you whether the bank provides check-cashing services for noncustomers. Banks normally don't provide bill-paying services, so you are left with purchasing money orders or cashier's checks for a fee.

The financial services market is rapidly changing due to technological advances. For example, a 7-Eleven clerk told me that she is paid with a prepaid card that she cashes at the ATM in the store. Alternative methods of getting your paycheck will continue to grow. However, the question is, "How much is a check-cashing and bill-paying method costing you, and how much is that cost taking from your paycheck?"

Bank Accounts versus Currency Exchanges

Given the previous discussion, the benefits of using a bank or credit union in general are greater than other methods available for cashing your check and paying your bills. This may change as technology continues to level the playing field and more companies look to provide financial services to those who are not currently using banks.

Benefits of a Bank Account and Relationship

There is an additional benefit of having a bank account. If you steadily increase the size of your savings account and properly manage your checking account to avoid overdrafts, the bank will begin to offer you other financial services, such as credit cards and car loans. In time, they will ask you if you need a mortgage loan to buy a house. You want the bank to begin making you these offers. Perhaps you will get a car loan from your bank, or maybe, through research, you will find a better interest rate or term somewhere else. But this progression is part of managing your finances so that you can do the things you want to do in your life.

Needed: A Computer, Internet Access, and E-mail Address

Most young adults today have mobile devices, and most of these mobile devices have Internet access. Smartphones, tablets, and laptops come in a variety of price points, but most are fairly inexpensive. If you are on your own, you need a smartphone and a laptop or tablet. If you are relying solely on a smartphone to take care of your financial and personal business, you will eventually need something with a larger screen. In the immediate future, you will be able to link your mobile device to the television monitor, in which case your mobile device will be all you need. Most new television monitors allow you to connect your tablet or laptop to the monitor so that you have a larger viewing area. In time, you will be able to connect your cell phone to your forty-two-inch or fifty-five-inch TV. At that point, you can do most things that you would on a tablet or laptop, depending on the apps available, which are many. There are now virtual keyboard devices for cell phones, which project a full-size, functional, virtual image of a keyboard on a flat surface. With this device, you can type a letter, or create a spreadsheet, or conduct any other activity that you would on a laptop or desktop computer.

Until then, you will need a laptop or tablet in addition to your cell phone to manage your finances and take care of your personal business.

Internet access is fairly accessible, and most companies now offer free Wi-Fi, although it is often not secure. If you depend on or use free Wi-Fi, you should get a virtual private network (VPN) app so that no one can read your e-mail or information while you use the Wi-Fi network.

With virtually all Internet plans, the Internet service provider will offer several free e-mail accounts. There are also free e-mail accounts from Google, Yahoo, and other Internet companies. Most companies, service providers, utilities, and financial institutions will ask if they can reach you via e-mail, so you'll need an e-mail address to take care of your personal business—and many of you may have one already. Once again, this is a low hurdle you can easily jump over.

Chapter 5: Getting Your First Apartment

Looking for an Apartment

It will be assumed for the sake of this chapter that you don't want to rent a room in someone's house. Although that is an option to consider, the focus here will be on getting your own place. In chapter 2, we discussed how to estimate the cost to move into a new apartment. Now let us discuss the process of finding an apartment.

The first question is, "Where do I look for apartment rentals?" In general, the following are methods to search for an apartment, and I will discuss each method in turn:

- Look for physical rental signs with contact information in the areas you want to live.
- Look on the Internet.
- Look in the apartment rental section of your local newspaper.
- Ask family and friends.

Look for Apartment Rental Signs

We have all seen these signs in our comings and goings. As you go to school or work, or as you are shopping or visiting, you will see "For Rent" signs on apartment buildings and houses. These signs will have a phone number you can call for information. This may not be the most efficient method, but if you see a sign on a place that looks interesting, call the number for more information. This works when you want to live in the area where you currently hang out. Nothing is stopping you from driving or walking around other areas you don't know as well and looking for rental signs, but this isn't the most effective method outside your own traveling circles.

Look on the Internet

The Internet is a great place to look for apartments using various sources. There are websites specifically for apartment searches. If you had no idea where to search, then you can search on the phrase "apartment rental websites." Of course, you can have a more specific search phrase to include your city or area code. For this example, here is what came up in a Google search using just "apartment rental websites":

Zumper - Apartments for Rent and Houses for Rent ...
https://www.zumper.com/ ▾ Zumper ▾
Find hundreds of thousands of homes and apartments for rent on Zumper. ... anyone else has seen it on other rental search sites like Craigslist, Zillow or Trulia.

Apartments.com: Apartments and Homes for Rent
www.**apartments**.com/. ▾
Find apartments, homes and condos for rent in your area. See real-time rental availability, costs and utilities included. HD videos, Hi-Res photos, pet policies ...

Domu | Chicago's Apartment Site
www.domu.com/ ▾
Search Chicago's largest apartment site and contact local landlords directly. Domu offers the best listings and makes finding and renting apartments easy.

Trulia: Real Estate Listings, Homes For Sale, Housing Data
www.trulia.com/ ▾ Trulia ▾
Your destination for all real estate listings and rental properties. ... real estate site that gives you the local scoop about homes for sale, apartments for rent. ...

Top Apartments for Rent - 805,000 Rentals by Apartment List
https://www.**apartment**list.com/ ▾
Welcome to the best apartment-hunting resource. ApartmentList.com. Our mission is to reinvent the rental market on a foundation of trust and transparency.

Beyond Craigslist: 10 Sites for Apartment Hunters - Mashable
mashable.com/2012/05/01/**apartment**-search-**sites**/ ▾ Mashable ▾
May 1, 2012 - Here are 10 sites to help you find the perfect apartment in your neighborhood of choice at your ... It includes rentals, condos and homes for sale.

There were more than five million results based on this general search phrase. You can go to any of these websites to see whether they will be helpful in your search. Zumper.com, for example, states that it has more than a million listings for rental houses and apartments. It also has a tool that will let you complete a rental application online (this may or may not be available for all the listings), as well as links to apartments in the major cities.

Apartments.com has a search engine on the first page that includes the city, minimum and maximum rent, and the number of bedrooms and bathrooms to target your search. It also has links to the major cities.

Using just this search method can get you started, and each website explains how to use its site. Within the Google search bar, there were other common phrases such as "best sites for apartment rental," "apartment rental search engines," and "Zillow and best apartment rental website." Many of these sites will include pictures of the apartment, which is a useful benefit.

With the Internet in general, the issue is not quantity but quality. You can find information, but you must use your judgment to discern the quality of the information. So this is one effective method for finding information.

Use the Local Newspaper Rental Section

Most local newspapers will have an apartment rental section based on the areas that the paper serves. In Chicago, for example, the two major newspapers are the *Chicago Tribune* and *Chicago Sun-Times*. These papers have an expanded Sunday edition that has a larger apartment rental section. There is also an independent paper called the *Reader* that many people use to search for apartments.

However, all three of these papers have an Internet website that you can access twenty-four hours a day for free. So we are back to the Internet. Let's assume you want to move to a city where you do not know the local newspapers. For demonstration purposes, I did a Google search on "Chicago newspaper with apartment rentals," but the results did not include the *Reader*. The search bar included the phrase "Chicago classified apartments," which came up with the following, more inclusive, results:

Classified - Chicago Tribune

www.**chicago**tribune.com/**classified**/ ▾ Chicago Tribune ▾
Find Chicago Tribune classifieds. Place an ad. ... Browse and post real estate listings.
Browse automotive classifieds. ... Automotive - Apartment & home rentals.
Apartments & Condos - Apartment & Home Rentals - Real Estate - Autos

Classifieds - Chicago Tribune

classifieds.**chicago**tribune.com/ ▾
PUBLIC HEARING NOTICE NORTH CHICAGO HOUSING AUTHORITY'S 2016 PHA
PLAN 2:00 PM, MONDAY, May 16, 2016 KUKLA TOWERS 1440 JACKSON ...

Chicago Reader Classifieds

chicagoreader.kaango.com/ ▾
Post classifieds ads and search classifieds ads in Chicago, Illinois for Chicago
Reader in General Classifieds. Jobs/Help Wanted. Entertainment, Services ...

chicago apartments / housing rentals - craigslist

https://**chicago**.craigslist.org/search/apa ▾ Craigslist Inc. ▾
chicago apartments / housing rentals - craigslist. ... Mar 10 HOUSE FOR RENT ! 4
BDRMS & 2 BATHS $1350.00 WILL ACCEPT A 3 BDRM VOUCH $1350 / 4br ...

The first link to the *Chicago Tribune* presents a search feature that includes minimum and maximum rent, number of bedrooms, city, state, and zip code, and radius. The radius lets you choose how many miles from the city or zip code you want the search to provide additional rental ads. A search for a two-bedroom apartment took me to a listing on the apartments.com website, so it appears that the *Chicago Tribune* is using apartments.com as its search engine. Most of the apartments had at least a picture of the outside of the building. Some listings had interior apartment photos, and in some cases, video clips as well.

Using the Internet, you can, in addition to researching the apartment, research the neighborhood if it is unfamiliar to you. So for many newspapers, it makes more sense to go to the website. If you don't have Internet access, you can buy the paper to do your research, or you can go to your local library and use a computer or read the paper.

Ask Family and Friends

There is a benefit to asking people in your family and social network about apartments. The reason is that you may have a chance to see an apartment before it is listed. Also, when you are introduced to the landlord, you have more credibility as being the daughter or son of a friend or church member. This is true unless you have a bad reputation, in which case they may not give you the contact in the first place. Getting an introduction through a family member or friend in most cases gives you an advantage over someone the landlord does not personally know.

This section discussed how to perform your search. The next section will discuss how to contact the landlord or rental agent and how to gather information to help you make a decision.

Evaluating the Apartment and Neighborhood

Now is the time to contact the landlord and make an appointment to see the apartment. You need to know and/or confirm the following information:

- How much is the monthly rent and the required deposit?
- How much are the utilities?
- Is there an on-site laundry room?
- Are there any other amenities (such as a fitness room)?
- Is parking available?
- Is it close to public transportation?
- Is there convenient shopping (grocery store)?
- Ask for a copy of the lease agreement.
- Ask for any written rules or policies for tenants.
- Get a rental application.

How much is the monthly rent and the required deposit?

If you did an Internet search, most likely the listing had a rental amount. Now you can confirm the information in the listing. If the listing did not mention the deposit, ask for the cost. Now you have the amount for the costs you estimated in chapter 3.

How much are the utilities?
The utilities will vary with each renter. However, there are average usage rates, and the landlord can provide you an average monthly cost. At this point, you can determine or confirm what utilities, if any, are paid by the landlord. If for some reason the landlord or rental agent cannot provide you with this information, then ask the utility companies.

Is there an on-site laundry room?
If an apartment has access to a washer and dryer, the listing will normally state this as an amenity (benefit). If the apartment has access to a washer and dryer, ask to see the room where it (they) are located and take note. Do you feel comfortable going there in general or in the evening? If the apartment does not have access to a washer and dryer, ask for the location of the nearest Laundromat. Then go visit it to determine if you would feel comfortable doing your laundry at this place. If not, check out another facility.

Are the any amenities?
Some apartments, typically the larger ones, may provide access to a fitness room, and some may have a swimming pool. Normally, these types of amenities are identified in the listing. When provided, you should look at them and make note of their condition. Are you paying a higher rent for something you will not use or you think is inadequate?

Is parking available?
If you have a car, does the apartment provide parking, or do you have to park on the street? If you have to park on the street, is there sufficient and safe parking available?

Is it close to public transportation?
If you don't have a car, is the apartment located close to public transportation? How long will it take you to get to your job?

Is there convenient shopping?

How far is the grocery store or pharmacy? Is there something in walking distance or a five- to ten-minute drive? If you are using public transportation, how long does it take to get to these facilities?

Ask for a copy of the lease agreement.

If you think you may want to rent the apartment, then ask for a copy of the lease agreement. It will tell you such things as which day the rent is due, the late fee, or how much notice they must provide you if they want to enter the apartment for repairs or inspection.

Ask for any written rules or policies for tenants.

Many apartment complexes have their own tenant rules and policies. Ask for a copy, and if it is a small apartment building or a duplex, ask whether there are any particular concerns they have that you should know about. Maybe the landlord does not want to hear music from inside your apartment after 10:00 p.m. Beyond the issue of whether someone's rules are legally enforceable, look to avoid any potential problems. It is better to become aware of an issue before you sign the lease and give the rental agent your money.

Get a rental application.

If you know you want to rent the apartment, then get an application to complete. If you are still researching, ask for the application just the same, as it will tell you what the rental agent wants from you.

Let's say you have decided on three apartments and want to make a side-by-side comparison. If you were to put this information in a spreadsheet, it might look something like this:

Monthly expenses	Apt. A	Apt. B	Apt. C	Comments
Apartment rent	$1,000	$800	$650	
Utilities				With some apartments, the rent includes utilities.
Electricity	$75	$50	$30	Averages.
Gas	$0	$100	$60	Gas included in Apt. A.
Cable	$0	$0	Included	Cable included in Apt. C.
Telephone	$60	$60	$60	Phone and data plan.

Food		$150	$150	$150	
Total		$1,285	$1,160	$950	
Parking	Yes	Yes	No		
Public transportation	No	Yes	Yes		
Laundry room	Yes	Yes	No		
Fitness room	Yes	No	No		
Convenient shopping	Yes	No	Yes		

With this information, you are able to determine how much it will cost you to rent an apartment. Also, if you ask the right questions, you can reasonably determine whether you are compatible with the apartment's environment and its apartment owners, your landlords. You can compare the cost of each apartment, along with its various amenities. This spreadsheet is just an example. It is not a full expense sheet like the one discussed in chapter 3. Also, this spreadsheet does not include the cost to get in an apartment, which was also outlined in chapter 3. It is simply an example of how you would create a spreadsheet to compare the apartments you are most interested in renting. All the cost information is just numbers to create a most-expensive and least-expensive apartment list with various conveniences so that you can compare them side by side and do some thinking in terms of what is important to you and where you can make trade-offs.

In summary, you can use the Internet and rental signs to locate apartments. On the Internet, most of the apartment websites allow you to look for apartments by location, cost, and size. Most listings also have pictures.

After contacting the rental agent to make an appointment to see the apartment, ask questions to determine the monthly rental costs, amenities, transportation, and shopping convenience. You can gather the cost information in a spreadsheet to compare your top choices so that you can decide where to submit an application.

You can do this analysis well before you are ready to move if you want to determine how much you need to save and how much an apartment costs to maintain. You can make some savings estimates based on how much you think you can pay, and as you get closer to having your cash ready, you can begin this process.

Chapter 6: Managing Your Money and Financial Tools—Part 2

Building a Credit History and Understanding Credit Reports

In addition to needing income at several points to manage your finances, you will need to borrow money through the use of credit to purchase such things as a new car and a home. Also, having a credit card in case of emergencies is an important tool. In fact, there are certain things that are difficult to do without a credit card, such are renting a hotel room or a car.

Even the most frugal individual in the modern age needs access to credit. One of the financial tools used by lenders to determine whether you are credit worthy is your credit report. According to the website myfico.com, a *credit report* is defined as "Information communicated by a credit reporting agency that bears on consumer credit standing. Most credit reports include: consumer name, address, credit history, inquiries, collection records, and any public records such as a bankruptcy filings or tax liens."

The three largest credit reporting agencies (also called credit reporting bureaus) are:

- TransUnion: www.transunion.com
- Equifax: www.equifax.com
- Experian: www.experian.com

When reviewing your credit report as part of a loan application, lenders will look at your credit history and your FICO scores. The website myfico.com defines *credit history* as "A record of how a consumer has repaid credit obligations in the past" and *FICO score* as "Credit bureau risk scores produced from models developed by Fair Isaac Corporation are commonly known as FICO Scores."

Every credit reporting agency will give a consumer a FICO score as part of the credit report. As someone moving out on your own, you are in the very beginning of building a credit history. You want to build a positive credit history that will support your efforts to live on your own.

By law, you are entitled to a free copy of your credit report from each credit reporting agency on a yearly basis. However, that report will not contain your FICO score. You have to pay extra for that information, which costs approximately twenty dollars. Because credit reporting agencies sell other products, such as credit monitoring and identity theft protection, they offer discounts when you buy other products. There are some services that provide credit scores for free, so you must do your research.

However, I suggest you get a copy of your FICO score if you plan to borrow money, because many lender websites will tell you what kind of interest rate you can borrow at a specific credit score range. If you don't plan to borrow money, then get the free credit report to review your credit history as well as other things being reported.

Sometime inaccurate information is reported about your history, and you can file a dispute with the reporting agency or contact the creditor that made the report to investigate. Also, as concerns identity theft, you can look for potential fraud on your credit report. If you see a loan being reported on your credit history that you did not take out, then you can make an inquiry. It may be possible that someone fraudulently took a loan out in your name, or someone with a similar name is being reported on your credit report by mistake.

It is a good idea to review the information on these credit reporting agencies' websites. In addition to increasing your understanding of the process, you will also learn how to repair your credit if you encounter a problem later on.

Borrowing Money
As mentioned in other chapters, you will face situations where you need access to credit. Credit is a useful financial tool. Let's briefly discuss the type of credit you may need to access in your process of living on your own.

Using Credit Cards
Having a credit card can help you when you have an emergency or are short on cash. There are different types of credit cards. There are general use credit cards, such as a Visa or MasterCard, which are the most flexible in terms of the places

you can use them. There are credit cards that you can only use at specific retail establishments, such as a retail store card or a gas card. Do not confuse credit cards with charge cards, such as American Express. Unlike credit cards, charge cards do not allow you to carry a balance and make payments; instead, the balance must be paid off completely each month. That's pretty easy when you have $25 on the card but not so easy when you have $500 or more. Be careful not to saddle yourself with this extra burden.

You need a source of income to get a credit card. To get your first credit card, you can apply with any lender you like. However, it is easier to get a credit card, such as a gas card or retail card, with a small limit. Some of these cards may give you a spending limit of a few hundred dollars in the beginning. This can get you started in terms of building the credit history that is being reported on your credit report. It is also a good way for you to learn how to use a credit card.

A credit card is basically a line of credit. That means that you are given a credit limit, for example, of $800. If you purchase something for $150, then you have a remaining available balance of $650. That new balance is the original balance of $800 minus your $150 purchase. Until you repay the $150, you only have access to $650. If you repay the entire $150 when it is due, and you have not made any additional purchases, then you have access to $800 again.

The usual mistake you must avoid is "maxing out" your card, which is spending the entire $800 balance and then only making the minimum payment each month. It is easy to buy things you don't need when you have extra money or credit. If you max out your credit card(s), then you don't have access to money in an emergency situation. Plus, making only the minimum payment every month keeps you in debt. There are many websites that explain the most effective use of credit cards, so my intent here is just to introduce you to the subject. There are many popular websites associated with various search engines, such as yahoo.com. However, for the sake of providing an example, let us do a search on the subject. The following are the top results for "how to use a credit card":

How to Use a Credit Card: 15 Steps (with Pictures)

www.wikihow.com › ... › Credit and Debit Cards ▾ wikiHow ▾
Part 2. Using Credit Cards Responsibly. Build your credit history with regular small purchases. Keep your balance low as possible. Avoid getting multiple cards at once. Guard your credit information carefully. Don't fall for exorbitant credit card offers.

How to Use a Credit Card Responsibly - Money Under 30

www.moneyunder30.com/how-to-**use-a-credit-card**-responsibly ▾
To use your credit card responsibly, you must develop the habit of paying your balance in full each month. That means keeping track of how much you're spending on your credit card each month and ensuring you will have enough cash the following month to cover your purchases.

Credit Card Basics: Everything You Should Know - Forbes

www.forbes.com/.../**credit-card**-basics-everything-you-should-kno... ▾ Forbes ▾
Jun 11, 2013 - The credit card is one of the most divisive products among all the financial ... of the user, a person with the power to choose how to use the tool.

Capital One Financial Education — Using Credit Cards ...

https://www.capitalone.com/.../**credit**.../**credit-cards**/using-cre... ▾ Capital One ▾
Whether you use your credit card to buy a computer or a cook book, good credit habits are essential to building and protecting your credit history. A credit card ...

Dos And Don'ts Of Using Credit Cards Wisely

credit.about.com › ... › Using Credit Cards › Best Credit Card Habits ▾
Guidelines for using credit cards the right way. Learn the way to use - and not to use - your credit card.

10 Reasons To Use Your Credit Card | Investopedia

www.investopedia.com/articles/pf/.../**credit-card-debit-card**.a... ▾ Investopedia ▾
Personal finance experts spend a lot of energy trying to prevent us from using credit cards - and with good reason. Many of us abuse them and end up in debt.

4 Things Credit Card Newbies Should Do to Establish Good ...

money.usnews.com/.../4-things-**credit-card**-n... ▾ U.S. News & World Report ▾
Jan 2, 2014 - If you're a first time credit card holder, follow these tips to build a solid ... Credit cards are great for building credit if you use them responsibly.

If you take the time to review several of these websites, you will gain an in-depth understanding of how to apply for credit and how to effectively manage your credit cards.

Although I searched on the phrase "how to use a credit card," other common search phases include:

- How to use a credit card wisely
- How to use a credit card to build credit
- How to use a credit card online

You have the option to look at the results of some of these other search phrases.

Car Loans

Unless you have access to several thousand dollars in cash, which the average reader getting started will not have, then you will need to get a car loan. In fact, you may need a couple thousand dollars in cash to get a new car, even if you do get a car loan. There are several things that affect your car loan search. The primary factor is whether you are buying a new or a used car. Also, in regard to a used car, it is also important whether you are buying that car from a major dealership (Ford, Chrysler, Chevrolet, Honda, Toyota, etc.), a larger used car company (CarMax or DriveTime), or if you are buying a used car from a small neighborhood car lot.

If you are buying a new or used car from a major car dealership or a larger used car company such as CarMax, then you will need to find a car loan through a traditional lender. All of these places have a finance department that will help find a car loan for you, but these finance companies are traditional companies that look at your income and credit rating. If you are building your credit history (as most of you are doing) and do not have any credit problems, such as poor payment history, most likely you can get a car loan, if you can clearly afford the car you want according to the finance department.

You can also look for a car loan that fits your needs on the Internet and go to the car dealership with a preapproved loan. To get further information on the car-buying and loan processes, let's look at a website search. Let me make clear that these are two different activities. Researching a car that fits your needs and then financing that car are two steps. Let us start with the search phrase "how to buy a car" (you can get more specific with "how to buy a new car" or "how to buy a used car"). Here are the results:

Eight Steps to Buying a New Car - Edmunds.com

www.edmunds.com/**car-buying**/10-steps-to-**buying-a-new**... ▾ Edmunds.com ▾
Feb 24, 2014 - 10 Steps to Buying a New Car on Edmunds.com: Learn how to locate,
price and negotiate your next new car.
Edmunds Price Promise - Negotiating Dealer Add-Ons ... - Car Shopping 101

How to Buy a New Car - Consumer Reports

www.consumerreports.org/.../**cars/new-cars/buying**.../i... ▾ Consumer Reports ▾
New Car Buying Guide from Consumer Reports provides new car reviews and ratings
with pricing to help you choose the best new car.
How to negotiate effectively - How Much Car Can You Afford? - Car Buying Surprises

10 Steps To Buying A New Car - Kelley Blue Book

www.kbb.com/**car**.../**car-buying**/step-1-know-your-sho... ▾ Kelley Blue Book ▾
Make car buying a pleasant experience by read and use 10 Steps To Buying a New Car
advice article to get the best deal on your next new car purchase.
Step 2: Narrow Down Your ... - J.D. Power Quality Ratings

How to Buy a New Car (with Pictures) - wikiHow

www.wikihow.com › ... › Buying and Selling Cars › New Cars ▾ wikiHow ▾
How to Buy a New Car. Let's say you've decided to invest in the new car or truck.
Sure, you can probably get a better deal with a used car, but you've probably ...

After researching how to buy a car, then you can start researching "how to get a car loan" or "how to finance a car." Once again, you can tailor the search to your specific situation. Let's look at the results of the phrase "how to get a car loan":

How to Get a Car Loan - 6 Steps to Auto Loan Success ...

blog.credit.com/2013/06/**get-a-car-loan**-66586/ ▾

Jun 3, 2013 - Try watching this video on www.youtube.com, or enable JavaScript if it is disabled in your browser. Step Three: Get Pre-Approved. You can shop for an auto loan online, as well as through a local credit union or bank. Step Four: Choose Your Vehicle. Step Five: Finalize the Paperwork. Step Six: Start Paying Your Car Loan.

9 Steps To Getting A Car Loan With Bad Credit | Bankrate.com

www.bankrate.com/.../**auto**/9-steps-to-a-**car-loan**-on-damaged-c... ▾ Bankrate ▾

Start close to home. "Even if you don't think you can get a loan, go to your bank, go to your credit union first," says Van Alst. Apply at the bank where you have a checking account or your credit union. And see if your employer or insurance company offers auto financing.

How to Finance a Car and Get a Car Loan | U.S. News Best ...

usnews.rankingsandreviews.com/**cars**-trucks/How-to-Finance-a-**Car**/ ▾

May 17, 2013 - A guide on how to get a car loan and what to look out for when financing a car. With a credit crunch squeezing everyone from General Motors ... The Basics - The Car Loan Term - Your Credit Score - Applying

Used & New Car Loan Financing Options - Wells Fargo

https://www.wellsfargo.com/**auto**-**loans**/.../**car-loan**-options/ ▾ Wells Fargo ▾

Financing your next new or used car can be quick and easy. Discover the benefits of working with us and find a vehicle loan option that may fit your needs.

How To Get Pre-Approved for a Car Loan on Edmunds.com

www.edmunds.com › Car Tips & Advice › Car Buying ▾ Edmunds.com ▾

Sep 29, 2015 - Getting pre-approved for a car loan makes negotiation easier, lets you know what you can afford and puts interest rates in perspective.

You should understand the process clearly by now. Go to these websites and do your research to determine the most effective way to get a car loan. As you can see, some of these websites are lenders, such as the Wells Fargo website, and some are finance related, such as Bankrate. With regard to performing more specific searches, you can research the following phrases:

- How to get a car loan with no credit
- How to get a car loan with bad credit
- How to get a car loan with no job

I mentioned small neighborhood car lots. It is often easier to get a car from these places for a couple of reasons. These cars are normally less expensive, and the car lot will finance you. In many situations, these places buy their inventory from car auctions where the fair market value, or "Kelly Blue Book" value, is more than what they paid for the car. They charge you a down payment that may cover their cost and give you a loan that is really what they are making in profit. As a result, it is easier to get a car from these places. The quality of the car will vary, and in many cases, these cars may not have a warranty. There are trade-offs in terms of easy financing versus car quality, but this is an option, if you need a car.

Yearly Federal and State Tax Filings

Federal Tax Filings

Now that you are working, you will need to file your income tax returns every year. You will have to file both a federal and a state tax return. If you get your income as a wage earner from an employer, then you will be provided with a W-2 form to evidence your income and the taxes you paid during the year. If you are a freelancer or contractor, then most clients will provide a 1099 form.

You will pay your federal taxes to the Internal Revenue Service (IRS), which offers a useful website: www.irs.gov. At this site, you can download all the forms and instructions you need to file your taxes annually. You can also file your taxes electronically on this site.

Another benefit of using the IRS website is that it provides free tax preparation software services called "Freefile." Free software is available from several IRS business partners if you make less than $62,000. There are numerous videos on YouTube discussing various aspects of the software and service. Just type "IRS freefile" in the YouTube search box for thousands of videos on the subject. This service also allows you to have your tax return directly deposited into your checking or savings account. There are also some free state tax return services available with some IRS partners. Go to the IRS website for more information.

State Tax Filings

Filing your state tax return is dependent on the state in which you live. There are websites that provide filing information for multiple states. In the state of Illinois, for example, you file your annual returns with the Illinois Department of Revenue (www.revenue.state.IL.US/individuals/filingrequirements). However, if you are not sure where to get information, as well as state tax forms in your state, then perform a search using the state name. For example, to determine how to file state returns for Michigan, type "state of Michigan tax filing requirement." Here are the top search results:

What are the State of Michigan income tax filing requirements?
www.michigan.gov/taxes/0,4676,7-238-43715-153718--F,00.... ▾ Michigan ▾
Taxes - Taxes Site ... should I do if I believe I am a victim of identity theft, didn't file a Michigan return but I received a 1099-G notice? ... Filing Requirements FAQs

Taxes - Filing Requirements - State of Michigan
www.michigan.gov/taxes/0,4676,7-238-43519_59553_69155-... ▾ Michigan ▾
Filing Requirements. Estimated Returns and Payments. Corporate, financial institution and insurance company taxpayers that reasonably expect to have a ...

Who Must File a Tax Return in Michigan? | Finance - Zacks
finance.zacks.com › Tax Information › Tax Filing ▾
The Michigan Department of Treasury recommends that any taxpayer in the state who files a federal income tax return should also file a Michigan return.

Geeks On Finance: Who Must File a Tax Return in Michigan?
www.geeksonfinance.com/info_7926941_must-file-tax-return-michigan.... ▾
For the 2010 tax year, Michigan's state income taxes are due on April 18, 2011. Most Michigan residents must file a state income tax return, but the state's laws ...

Tax Return Guidance for Nonresidents - Michigan ...
www.mtu.edu/..../tax/nonresidents-ret... ▾ Michigan Technological University ▾
Tax Return Guidance for Nonresidents. Federal Tax Information. Nonresidents who are

If you click on the first link, you will see that the Michigan Department of Treasury is the website from which to obtain tax forms, instructions, and other information.

In summary, accessing tax information is fairly easy. However, if you do not want to use the free services or do your own taxes, then you can go to a commercial tax preparer, such as H&R Block or Jackson Hewitt. There are dozens of tax preparation services that are fairly inexpensive.

Chapter 7: Transportation

In this chapter, we will look at the standard transportation options you will consider when moving out on your own. Some of your options are influenced by your location. There are places where public transportation is limited and not a viable option for you to effectively start and maintain your independence. However, most people want a car, because it is a convenient mode of transportation. You can come and go as you please and not worry about someone else's schedule. However, not everyone can afford to buy and maintain a car in the beginning. This becomes an income and expense issue. Thus, the standard options are:

- Using public transportation
- Buying a car
- Car Services: Uber and Lyft
- Getting a ride with someone else

Using Public Transportation

Using public transportation is significantly less expensive then owning a car. Some of you will use public transportation initially until you can increase your income in order to afford a car. However, public transportation is not as convenient as a car. Twenty-four-hour transportation, even with limited service between midnight and 5:00 a.m., is something most major cities will have available. But you have to live or plan to live in an area that has adequate public transportation. If there is inadequate transportation, you will have to get a car, unless you can get a ride from family, coworkers, or friends to get to work and the other places you need to go.

Once again, you can use the Internet to research available public transportation services, including travel schedules and pricing. I will use Chicago as an example. Chicago is a major city with twenty-four-hour public transportation services; thus, this level of service and information may not be available for a smaller city. The purpose of this example is to show you how to perform research on this issue so that you can make some informed decisions about availability and cost. I searched on the phrase "public transportation in Chicago," which yielded the following results:

Chicago Transit Authority - CTA Buses & Train Service - 1 ...
www.**transitchicago**.com/ ▾ Chicago Transit Authority ▾
The nation's second largest public transportation system provides rail, bus, and other transportation information for travel around Chicago.
Trip Planners - Transit Trackers - Maps - CTA Fare Information

CTA Trip Planners, Transit Directions - Chicago Transit ...
www.**transitchicago**.com/planatrip/ ▾ Chicago Transit Authority ▾
At the Chicago transit authority, we offer you two different ways to plan your tip with us ... a trips on transit throughout the Chicago area, including online trip planners, ... only accessible services, choose between bus, train, and multimodal trips.

CTA Maps - Bus and 'L' System Maps - Chicago Transit ...
www.transitchicago.com › Travel Info ▾ Chicago Transit Authority ▾
The CTA System Map shows both CTA Bus and Rail lines, as well as connecting services provided by other transit agencies in Chicago and surrounding ...

Chicago: Public Transportation - TripAdvisor
www.tripadvisor.com › ... › Chicago › Before You Go ▾ TripAdvisor ▾
Inside Chicago: Public Transportation - Before you visit Chicago, visit ... Metra provides convenient train service to/from downtown and many suburbs. They offer ...

Transportation in Chicago - Wikipedia, the free encyclopedia
https://en.wikipedia.org/wiki/**Transportation_in_Chicago** ▾ Wikipedia ▾
Mass transit in much of the Chicago metropolitan area is managed through the ....
Several intercity bus companies offer service to other cities in Illinois and ...

RTA Trip Planner | RTA, CTA, Metra, Pace, Driving and ...
tripsweb.rta**chicago**.com/ ▾ Regional Transportation Authority ▾
Plan your trip in Chicago and its suburbs using RTA, CTA, Metra and Pace, with ...
Chicago region using public transit (CTA, Metra, and Pace buses and trains) ...

Regional Transportation Authority
www.rta**chicago**.com/ ▾ Regional Transportation Authority ▾
RTA, CTA, Metra and Pace launch marketing campaign to get people to ride transit ...
and **transportation** agencies that support vital investments in public transit.

If you use the first link, it will take you to the Chicago Transit Authority website. Here, there is a tremendous amount of information about the bus and train system in Chicago. This website will tell you the schedules for various bus and train lines using the "Schedules" quick link. It provides maps, alerts, transit trackers, and fare information, and you can purchase tickets online using the Ventra app. You can also plan a trip, and there are how-to guides for those individuals who are new to the Chicago Transit System. This is just an example of the wide range of information available on the Internet.

Buying a Car

There are several issues related to buying a car, all of which you can research. These include:

- Buying a new car
- Buying a used car
- Leasing a car
- Getting a ride from someone else and carpooling

Buying a New Car

In general, buying a new car is a preference for most people. The maintenance costs for a new car are minimal in terms of getting the oil changed regularly and keeping the tires at the correct pressure. Plus, you have a warranty to take care of any major issues (which you should not have as a problem with a new car). So the main issues with a new car are the monthly payment and the insurance.

The monthly payment is a function of the price you paid for the car; therefore, you must buy a car that you can afford and that fits within your budget. Once again, this is the reason for keeping a spreadsheet of monthly expenses: you must determine how much you can spend on a car payment, insurance, gas, and parking. There is also the expense of registration fees and excise taxes associated with a car purchase. This is true whether you buy a new or used car or if you lease a car. Your budget is going to determine what type of car you are going to buy based on price—assuming you stick to your budget. It is tempting to buy a fast or beautiful car that you cannot afford, which is a sure way to put your independence at risk.

Keep in mind that most people upgrade over time. So given the money you have available, your first car might be a Nissan Versa for $14,000, but you can make the payments. If you manage that expense correctly for a few years, then you can get that larger, faster, and more stylish car you wanted in the future. However, for now, a new, inexpensive car that gets you to work and back without any problems is what you want. There are hundreds of websites that discuss how to buy a new car and that have a payment calculator to generate a monthly payment that you can put in your budget. So do your research, and refer to chapter 6 for a sample search of new car websites to research.

Buying a Used Car

In general, used cars are more expensive to maintain, depending on the age of the car. You can buy a used car, get a great deal, and not have any major problems. In general, however, maintenance is higher, and depending on the car's age, the original warranty may have expired and you must cover any repairs out of pocket. With age, a vehicle will have more problems, such as replacing aged parts as a result of wear and tear. However, used cars are cheaper than new cars, so the monthly payment is normally lower. In general, when you compare a new car to a used car, the new car costs more but will have lower maintenance costs, and the used car is cheaper but will have higher maintenance costs. In terms of your budget, the same financial issues apply. You must buy a car that you can afford and that fits your budget. If you want to research the issue, you can perform a search using the phrase "how to buy a used car," which will return the following results:

Eight Steps to Buying a New Car - Edmunds.com
www.edmunds.com/**car-buying**/10-steps-to-**buying-a-new**... ▾ Edmunds.com ▾
Feb 24, 2014 - 10 Steps to Buying a New Car on Edmunds.com: Learn how to locate,
price and negotiate your next new car.
Edmunds Price Promise - Negotiating Dealer Add-Ons ... - Car Shopping 101

How to Buy a New Car - Consumer Reports
www.consumerreports.org/.../**cars/new-cars/buying**.../i... ▾ Consumer Reports ▾
New Car Buying Guide from Consumer Reports provides new car reviews and ratings
with pricing to help you choose the best new car.
How to negotiate effectively - How Much Car Can You Afford? - Car Buying Surprises

10 Steps To Buying A New Car - Kelley Blue Book
www.kbb.com/**car**.../**car-buying**/step-1-know-your-sho... ▾ Kelley Blue Book ▾
Make car buying a pleasant experience by read and use 10 Steps To Buying a New Car
advice article to get the best deal on your next new car purchase.
Step 2: Narrow Down Your ... - J.D. Power Quality Ratings

How to Buy a New Car (with Pictures) - wikiHow
www.wikihow.com › ... › Buying and Selling Cars › New Cars ▾ wikiHow ▾
How to Buy a New Car. Let's say you've decided to invest in the new car or truck.
Sure, you can probably get a better deal with a used car, but you've probably ...

You can buy a used car from a new car dealership selling trade-ins, from a used car lot, or from an individual. If you buy the car from an individual, you will need to find your own financing if you are not paying cash. Like everything else, you can find and apply for car financing on the Internet.

Leasing a Car
A lease is nothing more than a long-term rental agreement. You can rent or lease a car for the weekend from a car rental company. But you can lease a car for three years from a dealership. You never own the car, you are only renting (or leasing) it. Some leases require you to buy the car at end of the rental term (open-ended) while some do not (closed-ended). Whether it is better for you to lease a car or buy a car will require that you examine each transaction and compare their benefits and drawbacks. There are websites that discuss how to make such comparisons such as edmunds.com and consumerreports.org.

Car Services

There are car services similar to taxi cabs such as Uber and Lyft that you can use as part of your transportation options. You have to look at the cost of being driven to various places to determine under what circumstances these car services are cost effective.

Getting a Ride from Someone Else or Carpooling

Some of you will have the option to catch a ride with someone else. However, this is not a long-term goal, because it can be inconvenient for you. It should be viewed as a short-term means to an end if the other options are not currently available.

Some areas are concerned about traffic congestion and recommend carpooling. So if you can join a carpool for work, without a car, by paying for gas that is an alternative. That may not help you with shopping and other errands, but it will provide you with transportation to work and help maintain your lifestyle while you work on getting yourself to a higher income that allows you to afford your own transportation.

Car Insurance

Car insurance is required in most states. You must check the requirements for the state in which you live. In Illinois, for example, you are required to maintain a minimum of liability insurance to cover a person you may injure in a car accident that is your fault. Per the Secretary of State office in Illinois, "You are in compliance with the mandatory insurance law if you have vehicle liability insurance in the following minimum amounts: $25,000-injury or death of more than one person in an accident. $20,000-damage to property of another person" (see www.cyberdriveillinois.com/departments/vehicles/mandatory_insurance.html).

Many individuals who are on a tight budget only maintain this minimum mandatory liability insurance. However, this insurance does not protect you in an accident. If you hit a tree or if someone hits you, your insurance does not cover your injuries and medical expenses. You hope or assume the person who hits you has the mandatory insurance, but this is not always the case. Therefore, you must consider getting an automobile insurance policy that covers you and your car in an accident. If you have medical insurance then having this additional medical insurance may not be necessary. If you don't have medical insurance, you have a potential problem if you are injured in an accident. If you are driving an older car that does not have many of the newer safety features, such as side door air bags, rearview camera, or radar warning, then that is another reason to consider full-coverage car insurance.

We all know that many people are distracted when driving by talking on the phone or texting or applying makeup in the rearview mirror or because they are tired, intoxicated, or just not paying attention. Plus, we all make mistakes, even under the best of circumstances. So consider full-coverage car insurance to protect yourself and your car. Once again, look at your budget to see if you can work it in, if not now, then later. If you cannot afford it now, this should be on your list of upgrades.

Parking

In some areas, parking can become a significant expense. If you work in downtown Chicago, for example, it can cost $20 a day to park in a parking lot. That is $100 a week, or $400 a month. That is a major issue for someone making minimum wage or even $15 an hour. So once again, try to determine whether parking is going to be a significant expense for you.

Chapter 8: Your Physical, Mental, and Emotional Health

The primary focus of this book has been on the practical aspects of moving out on your own. Living on your own involves a lot more than what is covered in this book. There are issues regarding nutrition, relationships, and other things that are beyond the scope of our current topic. However, I do want to discuss the need to take care of you. You need your health in order to function at your best. Like most things in your life, not only do you need to develop certain skills, but you also have to do things to maintain and enhance those skills. Developing, maintaining, and enhancing your health are part of an important skill set.

We are creatures of habit. You will develop some good habits that will strengthen you and some bad habits that will weaken you and undermine your success. Everyone needs to find some form of exercise or activity that they enjoy and that will keep their bodies healthy. Try out various activities to discover what suits your body, whether that is lifting weights, jogging, yoga, dancing, basketball, or something else that will keep you in shape. This activity is just as important as anything else I have mentioned in this book.

Being an adult and living on your own is stressful. If you grew up in a decent home environment, there were a lot of issues you never had to consider because your parent(s) had them covered. Now that you are moving out on your own, it is time for you to manage those issues. You will have moments when this responsibility will mentally and emotionally burden you. Physical activity can relieve some of the stress. However, you will have moments where you need something else beyond the physical.

Some people engage in daily meditation or pray and/or regularly attend religious services. Some are close with their families, and others have close friends as support. All of these things you can do in various combinations. But no matter the type of help, everyone needs mental and emotional support. If you have problems that appear overwhelming, seek help. There is a difference between being isolated and being self-sufficient. Take time to nurture strength of body, mind, and spirit. Like everything else in this book, you can perform research on the Internet and talk to people who have expertise in the things you need to know.

Finally, we need to feed our bodies—and if we feed ourselves the wrong things, we can become sick. But you not only need to feed your body; you need to feed your mind and spirit. You feed them with the things you read, the music you listen to, the people you associate with, and the programs you watch. Some of the choices you make in terms of content when engaging in these activities will strengthen you, and other choices will weaken you. Some choices will bring you joy, and other choices will depress you. You cannot control everything you see, hear, smell, taste, and feel. You cannot un-see what you have seen, but you can choose not to look at it again. As an adult, you make choices, and if you make the wrong choice often enough, it becomes a bad habit. There are lessons you can learn from making bad choices, but you don't need a bad habit. The point here is to stay mindful of the choices you are making and how these choices are influencing your life.

Chapter 9: This Is Only the Beginning

This book is about a transition and a new beginning. Living on your own is exciting and comes with a lot of freedom. It also comes with a great deal of responsibility and stress. You are now primarily responsible for taking care of yourself. However, this is a natural progression in everyone's life, and there are many more changes to come your way.

Right now, you are building a foundation for yourself. The skills you learn now and the habits you develop will serve you later in life. You will learn how to cope with changes, and some of these changes will favor you. In time, you will get a better apartment, and eventually, you will purchase a house or condo. In time, you will further your education, whether you get a formal education, such as a college degree, or you get a degree from the school of hard knocks. This book is an effort to assist you in a transition that is simply one of many you will face in your days ahead. Learn from your mistakes, because life is full of trial and error. Develop your skills and self-confidence. Good luck.

CPSIA information can be obtained
at www.ICGtesting.com
Printed in the USA
LVOW04s1604160117

521118LV00012B/1522/P